PRAIRIE TIME

NUMBER TEN:
Sam Rayburn Series on Rural Life,
Sponsored by Texas A&M University–Commerce
James A. Grimshaw Jr., Series Editor

PRAIRIE

TIME

A Blackland Portrait

MATT WHITE

Texas A&M University Press   *College Station*

The paper used in this book meets the minimum requirements
of the American National Standard for Permanence
of Paper for Printed Library Materials, z39.48–1984.
Binding materials have been chosen for durability.
∞

The map on pp. xii–xiii is used by permission of the Bureau of
Business Research, the University of Texas at Austin.

Library of Congress Cataloging-in-Publication Data

White, Matt.
    Prairie time : a Blackland portrait / Matt White.—1st ed.
    p. cm.—(Sam Rayburn series on rural life ; no. 10)
    ISBN 1-58544-501-0 (cloth : alk. paper)
    1. Blacklands (Tex.)—Description and travel. 2. White, Matt—
Travel—Texas—Blacklands. 3. Blacklands (Tex.)—Biography.
4. Natural history—Texas—Blacklands. 5. Prairie plants—Texas—
Blacklands. 6. Blacklands (Tex.)—Environmental conditions.
I. Title. II. Series.

F392.B546W48 2005
917.64'26—dc22   2005025898

CONTENTS

SERIES EDITOR'S FOREWORD

BLACKLAND Prairies have special qualities that James Conrad characterized in 2003 in a feature article on Matt White for the *Greenville Herald Banner:* "Most of the grasses found on the pastures and meadows of Hunt County, called exotics or hybrid, many imported from Africa, Europe, and Asia, are very different from the native, indigenous grasses found on the original treeless lands of Northeast Texas. These native grasses, some with root structures going sixteen feet deep, are hardy, drought resistant, requiring no fertilizers to flourish and support intense animal communities of insects, birds, and small mammals that are seldom found on cultivated pastures." Matt White's *Prairie Time: A Blackland Portrait* is a celebration, an account of his deep investment in his native environment, which he has studied and worked diligently to preserve.

Richly told, *Prairie Time* is a lyrcial inventory of the intricate world of native flowering plants, exotic grasses, trees, and other inhabitants of the Blackland Prairies. Drawing on his academic background in history, White describes the richness of the inheritance of these remaining treasures. His research about the region is extensive—early inhabitants, buffalo herds, the role of immigrants, individuals who have worked to protect prairie flowers and grasses—as are his personal field experience and observations. He is able to explain the natural cycles; the survival of grasses despite challenges from cultivation, overgrazing, building, and paving; the effects of the land on familial ties; and the richness and benefits of the Blackland soil. Readers will surely share his excitement and disbelief at seeing the Garrett family prairie, still intact, as well as his sense of loss over the Carolina Parakeet.

White gives an accounting of the winter magic on the prairie, the mystery within the wood prairie itself, the advantages of prairies as a hedge against drought, erosion, and stagnation, and their importance as a source for medicinal plants. He explores aesthetic value and he also offers historical perspective. The French, Belgian, and Swiss immigrants to Dallas, for example, brought an "infusion of intellectual capital"; a French botanist recognized the beauty and importance of natural plants in the White Rock Lake area, now in part an urban preserve. Through narrative, family stories, historical accounts, and personal observations, White guides us through the experience of a walk on a prairie.

Matt White is one of the environmentalists who have made a persistent difference in prairie conservation in this region. In 2003, the Cowleech Fork of the Sabine River Preserve—near the Dixon community south of Greenville—was tagged to become the newest Hunt County natural preserve. Other natural prairie lands include the Daphne Prairie, Clymer Meadow, Paul Mathews Prairie, County Line Prairie, and at least three others not yet designated and named. In Texas, Hunt County is second only to Lamar County in the amount of land designated as prairie preserves. Admitting that he has more to learn, White shares his abundance of knowledge and enthusiasm about the Blackland Prairies. His addition to the Sam Rayburn Series on Rural Life makes a significant contribution to our expanding knowledge of this region and our appreciation for the value of its hidden and ignored features.

—James A. Grimshaw Jr.

ACKNOWLEDGMENTS

First I wish to thank God for the beauty of his Creation and for eyes to see and ears to hear.

For introducing me to prairies, I want to thank my colleague David Montgomery of Paris Junior College. I am afraid that on numerous evenings I may have kept him from attacking the stack of papers that needed to be graded because I was sitting in his office asking questions about prairies.

James Conrad curates the archives at Texas A&M University–Commerce and has been extremely helpful in tracking down obscure references to prairies buried in the stacks and files under his care. I have no idea how many unsolicited packages have arrived in the mail from him containing photocopies of prairie material that might prove interesting to me.

I have been fortunate to meet and get to know a handful of prairie stewards—among them the Hicks family of Mount Vernon, Howard Garrett of Emory, Shelley Seymour of Dallas, the late Paul Mathews of Greenville, and Fran and Bill Woodfin for friendship and for taking me to Smiley-Woodfin Meadow. Without their devotion and passion for preserving this natural history, we would know much less about these beautiful treasures. Jim Eidson of the Nature Conservancy permitted access to Clymer Meadow and Triden's Prairie.

I would like to thank David Bezanson of Natural Areas Preserve Association for discussions about prairies and their conservation; Duncan Ragsdale and Graham Sweeney for the work they have done to introduce school children to prairies; and my good friend David Hurt for almost twenty years of shared natural history interests and pursuits.

I also would like to thank James (Bo) Grimshaw of Texas A&M University–Commerce for pursuing this manuscript for the Sam Rayburn Series on Rural Life. My editor Shannon Davies has proven unfailingly loyal and helpful and believed in this project (and me) from the beginning. Her optimism and enthusiasm are much appreciated.

My oldest daughter Natalie needs to be thanked for coming up with the title of this book when she was only three and her younger sisters Ellie, Riley, and Torie (my prairie girls) for the joy they bring. I also thank my loving wife Kristin for making everything possible. Finally, I would sincerely like to thank my parents Betty and Jack White for moving to the country before I was born so I would not have to grow up in a tiny backyard. They have not been thanked enough. Everything happens for a reason.

"When most people think of prairies, they probably recall images of the wide-open plains of Kansas or western Texas. The prairies of the Blackland Prairie, though, were quite different. These prairie fingerlings are not large flat plains extending from horizon to horizon. Instead-particularly in northeast Texas where dark alkaline soils mix with sandy acid soils-they are a complex patchwork of woods, brushy vegetation, and open grasslands. Many creeks and feeder streams (many of which are dry for months at a time) once bisected these prairies cutting them into pieces and laying out a pattern that was remarkably diverse and yet quite homogenous. Like alpine meadows protruding high above the timberline, these prairies were often growing on rolling hills and ridges, which slowly rose above the streamside woods."

PHYSIOGRAPHY

Scale

Source: Adapted from Erwin Raisz, *Landforms of the United States*, 1

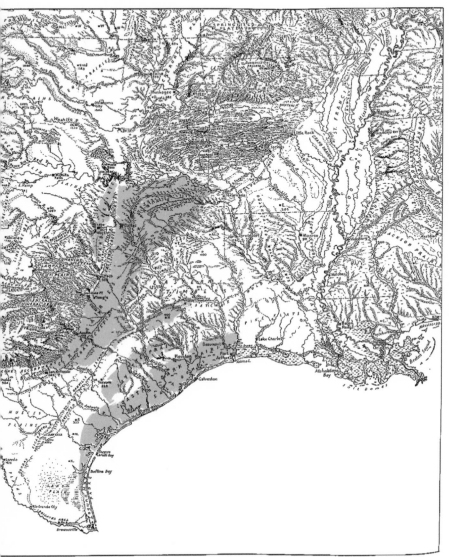

PRAIRIE TIME

INTRODUCTION

"I need more prairie time," complained our three-year-old daughter Natalie one evening as we drove away from the Paul Mathews Prairie in the half-light of dusk. We had brought her to the prairie for the first time that June afternoon as part of an experiment. Was she old enough to accompany us through the tall grass?

We need not have worried. She dove right in—literally—using both arms to part the tall grass. Her mother and I spent an hour looking at the flowers and grasses and teaching her what some of them were. As the last rays of sunshine turned the sky a wonderful palette of pastels, she was not ready to leave. "Can we spend the night here, Dad?" she asked.

Driving home in the darkness, I found that the words "prairie time" kept turning over and over in my mind. Something about those two words resonated within me.

Like a geological epoch, I realized, Prairie Time encompasses the countless eons when prairie grasses held sway before they were met by the advancing crush of civilization. Perhaps Prairie Time is also an attempt to reclaim that lost world through the fruits of imagination and intellectual understanding. The more I thought about it, the more I realized that Prairie Time is the mysterious lost world for which I have been searching by exploring prairies.

In Prairie Time, Texas' Blackland Prairie once stretched from near San Antonio north to the Red River near Clarksville. On the east it slowly graded into the Post Oak Savannah, and on the west it was replaced by the Cross Timbers—the westernmost flatland forests in North America. In a larger context, the Blackland Prairie was part of a much wider ecosystem called the Tallgrass Prairie that once thrived on the eastern edge of the Great Plains, all the way from Canada south to Texas. This ocean of grass was nourished by abundant rainfall in parts of the year and by humidity siphoning north from the Gulf of Mexico.

The Blackland Prairie was also the largest of a series of wide tallgrass prairie openings in the eastern half of Texas that are mostly surrounded by forest. When the French explorer LaSalle came ashore in 1684, an extensive prairie rimmed the Gulf of Mexico, extending inland for many miles. Other adventurers, as well as land-hungry explorers, would find other large prairies tucked away like inland seas of grass. The smallest of these inland seas was the Fayette Prairie, stretching from Gonzales northeast toward Walker and Montgomery counties. Farther north and west they found the San Antonio Prairie, which reaches from the eastern tip of Bastrop County to Leon and Madison counties. The extensive Blackland Prairie, which cut a vast grassy path across the state, was paralleled to the northwest by the Grand Prairie stretching from Johnson County due north to Cooke County.

These grasslands were all characterized as tallgrass prairies, which separated them from shortgrass prairies in the western United States where rainfall totals do not support such lush growth. Today tallgrass prairies exist mainly in the imagination, although a few postage stamp–sized preserves protect the last remaining examples of this once widespread landscape. By some estimates less than one tenth of one percent of Texas' 12 million acres of Blackland Prairie remain untouched by the plows that brought bread and butter to the families who settled this region. Most of these patches of prairie, as the unplowed remnants are called, survived because they were tucked away and were used as hay meadows by folks who valued native grasses as winter forage for cattle. A small percentage also remained because they sprouted out of rocky ground too stony to plow. Calling them prairies, though, is like calling a fingernail clipping a person; but since they are all that remain of these vast grasslands, they must serve as our prairies.

When most of us think of prairies, we probably recall images of the wide open plains of Kansas or western Texas. The prairies of the Blackland Prairie were quite different. These prairie fingerlings never were large flat plains extending from horizon to horizon. Instead—particularly in northeast Texas where dark alkaline soils mix with sandy acid soils—they were a complex patchwork of woods, brushy vegetation, and open grasslands. Creeks and feeder streams (many of which are dry for months at a time) carved these prairies into pieces, laying out a pattern at once remarkably diverse and yet quite homogeneous. Like alpine meadows protruding high above the timberline, these prairies were often growing on rolling hills and ridges, which slowly rose above the streamside woods. The ridges typically begin in the apex of two small creeks and widen as they gain elevation. The pattern is repeated over and over again throughout the region and is still apparent, although the native grassy coverings have been stripped away. Again like alpine meadows, these prairies once exploded with a riot of colorful wildflowers and grasses. From flowers that bloom barely above the ground to others ten feet or more in height, the variety of plant life that existed within just a few feet was remarkable.

Today the tall grass that grew in the prairie is more misunderstood than ever. With machines from garden-variety lawn mowers to large-scale tractor mowers, Americans wage an eternal war against growing grass because we misunderstand the value of tall grass. Yet the irony is that early pioneer accounts are full of superlatives about the beauty of the tall grass that grew on the prairies. Dig through any historical archives on the Great Plains and it soon becomes obvious just what an impression these colorful creations had on early travelers. Even before Lewis and Clark wrote about the grasslands on their famous epic journey up the Missouri River in 1804, earlier accounts indicate just how much the prairies impressed those who saw them.

To visit one today is to walk on hallowed ground, a kind of holy grail for those who yearn to revisit the land as it looked before it was remade and reformed by the rushing onslaught of settlement. To stand on the crest of gentle prairie hill and watch the gray and green clouds of an April thunderstorm advance over flowers so truly wild, like they have for millennia, is to witness a drama more suspenseful than the latest blockbuster.

Prairies are powerful places, but to experience them requires spending time on them. You should spend time admiring how a prairie hillside sloughs off into the distance and how the sky slides down to greet it. You should study the shapes and the textures as well as the smells. You must get the prairie under your skin and under your fingernails, and in the soles of your shoes and between the toes of your feet, before you will begin to understand its power.

But truly to comprehend the power of the prairie, you should visit often throughout the year to watch how the seasons are conducted. You should come several times each spring when the green grass shoots barely protrude from the earth and the succession of blooms begins. You should see how June's yellow sunflowers mirror the summer sun before being baked by it. You will want to see the prairie during the Indian summer of fall, when the deep blue skies are as wide as the prairie used to be and the prairie is transformed into a canvas of earth tones. Finally, you should also come when the chilling winds of winter render the prairie a starkly beautiful study in browns and oranges and frost adorns the dead flower stalks that stand out as somber silhouettes against a gray sky.

When you have seen the prairie this way, then you will mourn for its passing. When you learn to recognize a prairie by its plants, you will come to appreciate its uniqueness. When you get its scenery fixed in your consciousness like images of loved ones or little children, then you will seek the lost remnants that have remained here and there—forgotten and overlooked, as sometimes happens along railroad rights-of-way, in cemeteries, and on rocky outcroppings.

Once you learn to hear the prairie you will realize that it speaks in a strong, yet subtle, voice. Sadly, it is a voice drowned by the rhythms of car stereo speakers and the constant drone of automobiles, airplanes, and any number of other sounds, the noises of our economic and material success. Where silence is still allowed to reign, visitors may not appreciate the whispered tones of the prairie. To hear the timeless voice of the prairie, grab a handful of prairie grass and hold it above your head. Listen to the wind as it moves through the awns and seeds of the switchgrass. Watch how the linear blades of pastel Indiangrass are twisted and turned by the breeze. This is the voice of the prairie as it was borne by millions of blades of grass, each one a vibrating reed—a vocal cord—the wind's vocal cord.

Interwoven tightly within the fabric of this abused and worn-out land are countless stories of the people who wrestled a living here. Many of the stories are forgotten and many more are untold; I feel fortunate that I was allowed to hear some of them.

Most were told to me by my paternal grandmother, an indomitable mother of seven, born in 1893. I realize now that what she provided to me was a vital living link to a lost world, an early time in our history when the goal of life was simply to survive. Though I have forgotten some of them, her stories still echo inside me. I hardly go a day without thinking of her and of them. I suppose they are in a sense a living legacy, a tribute to her and her world and the people who shaped her character.

Yet one of my most insightful glimpses into the world of those people comes not from something she told me but from something she gave me. It is an old stained and torn photograph that dates to around the time of the Civil War. It was taken on the prairie of western Hunt County, near the small community of Clinton, and contains images of my father's grandmother and grandfather (before they were married) as well as their families. My grandmother's grandfathers are both pictured, men who were born during the first half century of the nation's existence and whose determination to forge west in search of a dream called Texas made them like so many other restless Americans who went in search of their own destiny on the tall-grass prairie.

She often told me about her grandfather, who came to Texas, bought land, and then donated some of it for the first local cemetery and for the first train at that same small community of

Detail of a Civil War–era photograph taken in Clinton, in western Hunt County, depicting both sides of my maternal grandmother's family.

Clinton. It was a story that made her proud. I sensed this every time she told it.

In the summer of 1985 after I graduated from high school, I took my camera and paid a visit to that cemetery. Before then my only real memories of it were of driving past when I was a child. But I had never had the freedom to look around at leisure. I realize now that I was on a mission to discover something deeper. Not having an unlimited budget to snap photographs and develop film, I chose my images carefully. I got photographs of the gateway, a panorama of the old headstones rising out of the knee-high grass, two images of the monuments—and a pink wildflower I did not recognize.

I placed the developed images in an album and over the next almost twenty years, I pulled them out only rarely. During the course of writing this book I again pulled them out and realized that of all things, the cemetery must have been much as my grandfather saw it. The pink wildflower is a relatively rare wild orchid called the Oklahoma grass pink orchid. In fact, not only was it not known from Hunt County (to the botanists who keep track of this sort of data)—it was not even described to science in the summer of 1985 when I photographed it! It would be another decade before University of Texas graduate student Douglas Goldman would realize its uniqueness. To me it is a small gift left by my great great grandfather in 1860 when he donated the cemetery and dug its first grave. I have no idea if the plant is still there—the cemetery is kept closely mown these days—but I have a feeling it is.

If I have come to any conclusion it is that prairie figures prominently in my existence. What I have come to realize is that I come from prairie people. Therefore it is with mixed emotion that I write about these people, the world they inhabited, and the way they treated the land around them. I may not agree with the choices they made, but I realize that those choices were often desperate ones meant to ensure their survival.

I realize also that I would likely have made the same choices given the same circumstances. We all would. The will to survive and to wrest life from the earth is something we all share, no matter how far removed from or unaware of it we are.

FOR THE SEA AS A WHOLE, the alteration
of day and night, the passage of the seasons, the procession
of the years are lost in its vastness, obliterated in its
own changeless eternity.

Rachel Carson, *The Sea around Us*, 1951

CROSSING THIS STREAM [the Trinity River
in 1835], we entered, on rising the western bank, the first large
prairie we ever saw, stretching further to the west than the
eye could reach. It is hard to describe the emotions of the soul
on looking for the first time across a vast prairie.
The feeling is somewhat akin to that experienced on the
first visit to the beach. Land and water there bore
some resemblance.

Z. N. Morrell, *Flowers and Fruits in the Wilderness*, 1872

INGREDIENTS

Attempts to compare what was once the immense and overwhelming tallgrass prairie with the vastness of ocean are not new. From the first Europeans who beheld its awe-inspiring power to those who have celebrated its majesty with written words, the prairie continues to be a figment of pelagic imagination. The simile survives and recurs because, quite simply, there is no better one. The prairie was an ocean of grasses. And just like the ocean, it was misunderstood—feared even.

Yet in one crucial way the prairie was different. It was erasable. It was voidable. It was in the end no greater than the sum of its parts. And once those ingredients were taken away, one at a time, it collapsed inward into the bowels of the earth from which it had come and then vanished like a sinking ship, perhaps forever. The ingredients that went into the fragile ocean of grasses called a prairie may seem simple enough, but the recipe itself was complicated and not well understood because it was mixed thousands of years ago. Apparently the prairie resulted from a unique interaction of at least five basic ingredients: grass, soil, fire and its antagonist, rain, and the beastly ruminants of the prairie—buffalo.

But once the prairie recipe was mixed, the careful blend of ingredients required perpetual care, like the maintenance needed to keep the engine of a car running smoothly. Take away oil and the engine soon overheats and is destroyed. Take away the fuel and the car eventually slows and comes to stop. A final element—often overlooked—that seems to have played a role in the existence of the prairies was the Native Americans whose own self-serving practices helped keep the grassland in running order.

Of these ingredients required to keep the prairie running, three have been removed forever. The result is the wholesale loss of a vast and beautiful landscape. Although the American Indians knew how to use and benefit the prairie, the Anglo Americans found there was no welcome mat on the edge of the prairie. There was no sign that said you are now entering one of the world's most complex ecosystems. No manual provided instructions on how to keep it alive. And so it vanished in the hands of a civilization whose concepts of wilderness were not big enough to encompass something so large as a prairie.

GRASS

As for man, his days are as grass: as a flower in the field, so
he flourisheth. For the wind passeth over it, and it is gone;
and the place thereof shall know it no more.

King David, Psalms 103: 15–16

A child said, What is the grass? fetching it to me with full
hands: How could I answer the child? . . . I do not know
what it is more than he.

Walt Whitman, "Leaves of Grass," 1855

SINCE before I was able to walk I have roamed grassy pastures. My dad would put me on his shoulders and away we
would go. Walking across our farm was a form of relaxation, and
perhaps even entertainment, for my parents, who insisted that
television not be part of our home. Until I was about three years
old I was hoisted to that much better vantage point whenever
the grass became too tall or the going got too tough. I enjoyed it
up there, though I think my dad was not as fond of it, especially
when I fidgeted or held on too tightly.

*The Blackland Prairie in its original condition was a complex patchwork of
woods, brushy vegetation, and open grassland.*

As I got older I had to walk by myself when we roamed our farm looking for breaks in the barbed-wire fences, a newborn calf, or pieces of carelessly discarded binder twine from a hay bale. When the grass was brown in winter, I learned, wearing socks would attract the sharp daggerlike seeds of a plant we called spear grass. These little weapons had the annoying habit of working their way into my shoes and socks and then into my skin, causing enough pain that they were impossible to ignore. On many occasions I would pause—often standing on one leg—to pick them out before running to play catchup. I later learned that this widespread grass was called three-awn, because of its three hairlike fibers called awns, and that it was common in overgrazed fields.

Now that my wife, Kristin, and I live on the farm where I grew up, we take our four daughters for walks as we follow in my parents' footsteps. I see myself in our children's actions, and my dad in mine. Natalie loves to be hoisted onto my shoulders where she can see the world like a grownup. Ellie is fiercely independent and insists on walking whenever we are on the dusty lane that winds through the farm. She is small though, so for her to see over the knee-high grass I must put her on my shoulders.

If settlers in the East encountered forests so dense that it was hard to see the forest for the trees, when they reached the Blackland Prairies they may have found it hard to see the prairie for the grass. In some places the prairie grasses grew so tall that to see across them required a man to stand on horseback. What must have looked to these people like a seamless sea of grass was actually a diverse mosaic of grassland communities.

Community is a term ecologists use to describe a habitat on the basis of the most common trees, grasses, or forbs that grow there. Just as a forest of pine trees is quite different in appearance from a forest of palms or oaks, or some mix, so grassland communities appear distinctive based upon what grows most commonly. Ecologists call these plants the dominants, and within the Blackland Prairie there are several such communities.

Our misunderstanding of the prairie is still evident in the way we use language to describe our experiences there. When prairie enthusiasts speak to each other about visiting a native prairie we always describe ourselves as being *on* the prairie. But to know the prairie you have to go *into* it—the same way you would go into a forest. Likewise, no one ever mentions standing on the woods because they are not two-dimensional. A healthy native prairie has height and structure and is thus three-dimensional, but to see this requires us to look a little more carefully—to change our perspective and our way of thinking.

While we tower over many of the plants that grow on the prairie, the prairie grasses must seem to a cotton rat like giant redwoods, and the tunnels rats create among the dead litter are like trails through a dense, lush jungle brimming with moisture. Instead of trees, the prairie grasses and flowers provide height and shade, preventing the sunlight from reaching the ground. In reality, a prairie is a miniature forest—a small-scale old growth forest. Growing from roots that are truly ancient, the grasses grow, mature, and die each year. This is the same cycle of life that exists in a forest, except that most of the forest's trees do not always regenerate from roots. If the grasses are the trees of the prairie, then big and little bluestem, Indiangrass and switchgrass, were once its giant redwoods. These tall grasses were called the "big four," and they dominated the tallgrass prairies from Texas to Canada while many of the other grasses and forbs lived in their shadow.

The distribution of these tallgrass communities is often related to the soil and the amount of moisture. There is disagreement among prairie ecologists about just how many different communities exist in Texas—some recognize five while others count seven. The most recent scholarship on the subject recognizes five grassland communities within the confines of the Blackland Prairie, with little bluestem being the dominant over the vast majority of the region and a dominant grass in three of the five communities. The dispute over the number of communities is minor and arises over whether grasslands where the next most common grasses differ should be considered distinctive communities.

Normally the smallest of the big four, and still the most common today even in old pastures, little bluestem is a delicate, erect grass that becomes washed with a burnt orange patina in winter, providing an appealing color contrast to the cyan of the sky—especially when it blankets an entire hillside. The narrow blades are light green in summer and the plant flowers in late summer. The seeds are easily dispersed by the wind, making this one of the first of the native grasses to return to a field when plowing ceases. Often called sage grass by local ranchers, little bluestem dominates on most prairies roughly south of a line from Greenville to Denton all the way to where the Blacklands dead-end near San Antonio. Its primary companions are big bluestem and Indiangrass in varying abundance.

Once more common than little bluestem across North American tallgrass prairies, big bluestem earned the pioneer nickname "turkey foot grass" because the three seed heads that rest atop the stalk when it flowers in late summer resemble the fowl's feet. The long narrow curly blades are light green, fading to orange-yellow in winter. The species was dealt a triple whammy when the prairies stopped burning, when they were plowed, and then when trees were allowed to grow. Widespread and regular plowing proved detrimental, but fire suppression too has played a key role in the receding of big bluestem from our landscapes. It is quite fond of flames and has decreased on prairies that are not burned regularly, although routine mowing on highway rights-of-way seems to have aided it by removing grasses that would crowd it out.

This grass, as I would learn, is also not particularly happy about being crowded out by trees. During a recent winter, workers hired by the electric company to guard the power line along our fence obliterated a narrow grove of mature post oaks. The trees were cut flush with the ground, including one large barrel-chested *Quercus stellata* specimen that must have been growing for many years, considering how slowly these stately trees grow. Later I was able to count nearly fifty rings in the cut-off stump of that tree.

In just a few minutes the chainsaw gang had turned the entire grove into a pile of firewood, while a giant tractor with a mower attached to a long hydraulic arm dispatched the smaller limbs and branches with the elegance of a stick of dynamite. Seeing these entire trees taken out, instead of the usual tree-deforming trimming job, caused a range of emotions, from anger to disappointment. Without any warning, this invading army had pushed over my fence (although the power lines are on the neighbor's property) and proceeded to leave an ugly swath of destruction. The workers seemed proud of the fact that their tractors would conquer any muddy conditions. Although we had received thirteen inches of rain in the previous forty-eight hours, they barged ahead, leaving two-foot-deep ruts all over the recovering grasslands on our land well away from what would be expected to service their right-of-way. The foreman's solution, he proudly exclaimed, would be to bring in a big tractor with a giant blade attached and smooth everything up as if the ruts had never happened. It would be all so simple; the grass would grow back, he confidently reassured me.

What he would not understand is that any scraping disturbance to the soil brings in a wad of unwanted weeds that thrive in the grassless vacuum created by the bare soil. Although I detested the deep ruts that scarred the land, his solution would be even worse. But the sadness that penetrated even deeper than the ruts was over the wantonness with which these people attacked the land.

For months I could hardly bring myself to walk that way— to return to the scene of the crime. It was only after a spring and a summer, with fall coming on, that I decided to salvage the firewood they had left, though it took some effort to muster the courage to go there. The ruts were still there, of course, but they were now mostly hidden by a green covering of grass. I also found that many of the stumps cut smoothly along the ground were suckering up, born again from life buried deep within the earth. But something else was present too, growing deliberately, exultantly, in the space where the oaks had been . . .

It was a moment of sheer wonder. About to burst forth in flower for the first time in perhaps a half century or more was a proud, majestic stand of big bluestem that covered an area the size of a two-car garage. Several small outlier populations, each with pencil-thin carmine red stalks sensual as lipstick, were attached to the fence like pearls on a necklace. The fence had saved them. And it is the fence that allows us to understand something of the history of destruction in this land. Imposed in the last days of Prairie Time, the fence had preserved a few scraps of native grasses that were under the barbed wires, sparing them from the plows that turned the land upside down.

But the fence also attracted the oaks, which came in from acorns perhaps dropped by birds and which began to shade out the mighty big blue. For decades as the oaks grew taller and broader, the grass spread its roots underground but was unable to gather enough energy from the sun to send up shoots or to blossom. Finally, freed from the shadows of the encroaching oaks where they had languished, patiently waiting for the trees to die, the grass roots were given the advantage by a chainsaw and, following ancient codes programmed into their DNA, were behaving as they once did.

This is a kind of patience that is hard to understand in our get-it-quick era of instant gratification. It is an ancient game between the grass and the trees, and unlike baseball or football games, it lasts more than nine innings or four quarters. It is a game fought over centuries between tough and resilient rivals. But the game can be played only when the grasses are still present, and sadly, today there is little left of them across much of the landscape.

Another stout, hearty native—and one of the big four—is Indiangrass, which sprouts pale bluish blades in spring and summer and adds a welcome contrast to the monotony of greens on the prairie. It is a beautiful grass with blue-green leaves the color of warm water in tropical seas. The golden seeds, which appear in late summer, are arranged at the top of the stem, forming clusters that wave in the wind and make the prairie look alive with movement. As winter's chill begins to the render the prairie a study in browns, the wide leaves fade to burnt orange— again adding a delightful contrast to the prairie.

Across the northern portions of the Blackland Prairie, mostly north of that imaginary line stretching from Greenville to

Denton, little bluestem takes a backseat to other grasses. Within the central heart of this region eastern gamagrass (thought to be a close relative of corn) and switchgrass become so common that they form a distinctive grassland community. Both thrive in moist soil with poor drainage and are especially fond of the ephemeral pools of water that form in depressions on the rich black soil.

During the spring and summer eastern gamagrass sports wide, leafy green, its leaves hinting at its mysterious relationship with corn. Unlike corn, though, its kernel-like seeds are not sheathed in shucks that must be removed before they can be planted but instead are perched atop tall reedlike shoots like the tassels of corn. Both male and female are represented in a single plant, a trick that must surely help this plant reproduce.

When eastern gamagrass falls under autumn's influence, its long leaves dry and curl and then, relaxed, array themselves outward in a circle, creating a most unusual floral spray. Its rough, masculine leaves become weathered with an earthy sepia tone complemented by a subtle wash of lavender-rouge—giving the plant a feminine appearance that is further suggested by its long hairlike blades, which fall all around it. The contrast is interesting considering that each plant is both male and female. It is a sight that should be seen by everyone who may have trouble understanding how someone could fall in love with a grass. When it still covers a prairie hillside, the effect is overpowering. Even the appearance of an odd plant here or a small patch there that somehow survived along a fence or in a cemetery or some similar situation can be powerful. Unlike the masses—the more democratic grasses that thrive anywhere under any circumstance—eastern gamagrass has a nobility that soon becomes apparent.

Switchgrass is the most unkempt of the big four. When flowering it resembles exploding fireworks, and it keeps this appearance from the time its tiny seeds mature in midsummer until late winter. Because the seeds germinate easily, switchgrass has become the grass of choice for many would-be prairie restorationists who restore without regard for what once existed in the area. A giant variety that once thrived in wet environments out west has become especially popular for use on highway rights-of-way and by land managers wishing to grow a monoculture of native grass for hay. In these circumstances switchgrass is sometimes quite aggressive, smothering other grasses and behaving like a weed.

On the eastern periphery of the prairie, where the rich black soil begins to yield to sandy clay loam soil and post oak trees, the prairies are dominated in early spring by a plant called Mead's caric sedge. Its dominance is an anomaly on the Blackland because this plant is not a grass at all. Resembling and related to nut sedge—the bane of every flower gardener—Mead's caric sedge is abundant on sandy prairies in the northern tip of the Blackland Prairie, strongly identified with the community that bears its name. To appreciate its butter-yellow pollen-laden blooms, which appear early in spring when young shoots of grass are just beginning to stretch their arms after sleeping underground all winter, you must get down on your hands and knees and peer into the prairie.

After this sedge stops blooming, Silveus's dropseed—called wire grass by pioneers—takes its place in the perennial succession that has played out on the prairie for thousands of years. Its name comes from the stout baling wire–like stalks that bear the seed heads two or three feet into the air. Its blades are the narrowest among all the large grasses, usually no wider than boiled spaghetti. Where this is the most dominant grass, it forms dense clumps that blend together like a floor full of green pompoms tossed aside by cheerleaders. It rules with such efficiency that even little bluestem and big bluestem have to receive permission to coexist alongside it. Where it takes a back seat to other grasses, it forms small cliquelike clusters that huddle together for safety.

For a long time I thought this community had once existed on the land where I grew up. Although I had not found it growing on the property, or even nearby, I assumed that since the soils where it is most common are similar to the Wilson sandy loam on our farm, it must have been here as well. This concern was more than merely academic to me. If I were going to attempt to restore the grasses, I would need to know what grasses should be restored.

Part of my reasoning, I suppose, was based on my mistaken notion that eastern gamagrass was mainly associated with the blackest clay—a soil not found on our farm. I began to cast my net a little wider and to explore for prairie remnants where they might be found, instead of where the books said they were. Incredibly, in the process, a clearer picture began emerging of the true diversity and distribution of local prairie communities. My searches took me down miles of back roads, where I began mentally mapping the distribution of forgotten prairie remnants and even individual grasses or single plants growing in roadsides or along railroad tracks. These sites, when compared with local soil maps, allowed me to get a better feel for just what grasses grew where, including eastern gamagrass.

What I learned was that eastern gamagrass extended well into the sandy loam soil and was not restricted to the dark clay. A serendipitous discovery came one winter day when I found a few clumps of eastern gamagrass and switchgrass right down the road from my mailbox, less than a quarter mile from my property line. The following fall I was even more surprised to find a larger population of eastern gamagrass beside an old cemetery, not thirty yards from my back fence.

I stood gazing in utter amazement one damp overcast October day at the answer to a question that had put me to sleep on countless nights, as I lay in bed contemplating whether eastern gamagrass belonged on my land. It was a serious question that had really bothered me, and I realized it was a question for which no library in the world would contain an answer. Later, the answer to that question was discovered quite remarkably by chance.

After about five years of unseasonably dry weather, a number of trees on our farm, all of them species not well adapted to drought, succumbed to the lack of deep moisture in the soil and died. Water oaks were the hardest hit, including several that were over fifty feet tall and almost two feet in diameter. What had attracted my attention when I found the eastern gamagrass that day was a dead water oak, which, characteristically, had already turned black and had broken at the base and fallen over. Under where its shadow had been was a healthy population of eastern gamagrass ready to thrive again. Somehow it had survived both the onslaught of the plows and the invasion of trees.

Invasive weeds provide yet another challenge to the prairie. Because the soil has been plowed so often and overgrazed by cattle as well, most of the native prairie plants have vanished. Plowing the soil year after year destroys the roots that tunnel deep into the ground searching for the moisture that will sustain them through the dry summer months. What has returned is degraded grassland called a pasture, a combination of mostly non-native grasses and invasive weeds. Our farm is covered with them. Botanists recognize no such thing as a weed; this word is simply a definition we give to any unwanted plant. Several times well-meaning friends have remarked to me that some native plant I have planted in my garden is "just a weed." It is all a matter of perspective.

One of the biggest threats facing prairie managers is keeping exotic grasses and flowers from becoming established. Not only do they change the original composition and look of the prairie; they often eliminate or outcompete native species. Many of the wildflowers that we admire so much as we drive down the highway are aliens, brought in by agriculture, the highway department, or wildflower enthusiasts. In fact, a large percentage of the flora of the Blackland Prairie is alien.

One of the most ubiquitous and obnoxious alien grasses is Johnson grass, a native of Turkey that was brought into the United States, possibly in 1835, by a man named John H. Means, who would later become governor of South Carolina. He planted some seeds from Turkey on his farm and later claimed the giant grass had spread to such an extent that no one wanted to buy the land. In 1840 a southerner named Colonel William Johnson—for whom the grass is named—planted some seeds that he had gotten from Means on his farm near the town of Selma, Alabama.

Others continued to plant the seeds—some apparently for birdseed and others for hay—causing Johnson grass to spread quickly. The Civil War may have aided its dispersal throughout the southern United States as hay was shipped to provide feed for horses. Johnson grass grows faster than most prairie plants, spreads via tough roots and underground rhizomes, and is easily spread from seeds. Today it is widespread and particularly fond of the Blackland Prairie. It seems to thrive in disturbed habitats such as roadsides, plowed fields, and old pastures.

Bermuda grass is another Old World pest. Of African origin, it was brought to this continent in the bedding of slave ships in the eighteenth century. It is an aggressive plant, a trait that makes it a popular lawn cover. Varieties of it are also used for hay meadows, but it also spreads rapidly and creates a mat of vegetation that soon chokes out native grasses and forbs.

An especially obnoxious alien is tall fescue, a European species introduced as hay and winter forage for cattle because it remains green during the coldest season of the year. Like many invasive plants, it spreads easily and has become a problem on native prairies. At the Nature Conservancy's Clymer Meadow Preserve in Hunt County, tall fescue has become such a problem that manager Jim Eidson has been working for years to remove it, using a variety of methods, including carefully applying herbicide to the plants as well as grazing and burning in winter.

King Ranch bluestem is another exotic that spreads rapidly and has become a problem grass. It took a circuitous route from China to California to Texas, where it was introduced in 1924 at Angleton. In 1937 it was discovered growing on the South Texas ranch for which it was named. Like tall fescue, KR bluestem was later promoted by the United States Department of Agriculture Soil Conservation Service and the Texas A&M Agricultural Extension Service as a means of erosion control.

Once the prairies were plowed and the tough grass roots were removed, the rainfall began washing the prairie sod away. In many places huge gullies and washes were formed as rainwater runoff carried away soil that had built up over thousands of years. Another particularly troublesome side effect occurred during the dust bowl days of the 1930s when the bare soil dried up and was blown away by the wind. Although the introduced grasses were seen as a miracle cure, today large areas of the Blackland Prairie have been stripped of native vegetation, which has been replaced by these and other introduced grasses and forbs.

The introduced species are especially threatening to the native biodiversity of the region. Grasslands that once harbored hundreds of species of plants per acre have been reduced to only a handful of species within the same space. With the removal of native plants, hundreds of other organisms—such as butterflies and moths—that were dependent upon the mix, or on a particular species, are also threatened.

Many areas, including some that are prairie, are infested with Queen Anne's lace, which bears attractive lacy white flowers. This introduced member of the carrot family has become a common wildflower in the state's largest tract of unplowed prairie, the 2,100-acre Smiley-Woodfin Meadow located on U.S. Highway 82 in Lamar County. I accompanied Jim Eidson and Bill Carr, a top-notch botanist employed by the Nature Conservancy, one summer morning as they inventoried plants on this sizable hay meadow. In June, when a half dozen yellow sunflowers should have been commanding attention, the parasol-like flowers of Queen Anne's lace, which many people may mistake for a native species, was stealing the show.

As we crossed the median in the four-lane divided highway that separates the Nature Conservancy's ninety-acre Tridens Prairie and several smaller unprotected prairies from the Smiley-Woodfin Meadow, we were amazed at how common an alien plant called pincushions has become. Adorned with round lavender flowers—like pincushions—this tall plant was introduced recently into the Dallas–Fort Worth Metroplex as a garden plant to attract butterflies. A native of Europe, it has begun colonizing the surrounding countryside with the force of kudzu in the Southeast.

We pulled as many of these plants from the ground by their roots as we could carry to keep them from spreading into the virgin soil nearby, though ultimately our efforts will likely prove futile. Because a roadway runs through them, these prairies are especially vulnerable to encroachment by aliens. Seeds are easily spread in several ways, particularly via the tractors and mowers that groom the right-of-way and by the highway department, which sows wildflower seeds across the state without regard for landscape integrity.

SOIL

....

The soil of the high prairies is very black and deep. Some
of the prairies it is true are of a grayish soil, which generally
produces badly—some of them are singularly listed with
narrow streaks of yellow clayish soil. . . . This black soil is
generally of a still waxy nature and but badly adapted to
stand the droughts.

Josiah Gregg, *The Diary and Letters of Josiah Gregg*,
July 17, 1841

When it rains here, as it has done last night and today,
there is no getting about at all, the mud is not like anything
you ever saw. It is perfectly black, and sticky, and when you
once get it on boots or pantaloons there is no such thing as
getting it off. There it will stay until it wears away like tar,
to which it is frequently compared. And heavy like lead.

Thomas Howell, Letter to his brother, September 17, 1852

BOTH my sets of grandparents are buried in the same Blackland Prairie cemetery outside the Hunt County town of Caddo

*The sacrifice of the old made way for the new and gave life to the prairie in
return.*

Mills. The first to go was my mother's father, who passed away a few years before I was born. I never met Pappy, as he was nicknamed, but was taken instead to see his marker on the few special occasions when we took flowers. The only relief was the hodgepodge of stones of varying shapes and sizes placed pellmell on the flat ground. In the middle was a worn-out octagonal pavilion that was once used for graveside services.

My mother and her parents were born on the tallgrass prairies of southeastern Kansas. As World War II loomed on the horizon my grandparents divorced. Pappy would marry a woman whose family had deep roots on the Blackland near Caddo Mills, bringing my mom and her sister to live here. This was where, following the war, she met and fell in love with my dad, who had just returned from a stint in the South Pacific.

Sometime around my twentieth birthday I realized that the common thread bringing both sides of my family to Texas had been this dark soil. The realization came as I was leaving the graveside funeral service of my aunt, who is also buried in this cemetery in the same soil that my dad told me so many times he hated. His complaints about it are nearly universal to Blackland dwellers and echo strongly the sentiments expressed by young Thomas Howell, who settled in the area in the early 1850s. After a rain, the black gumbo soil becomes wet and sticky and behaves like snow on a snowball being rolled across the yard. Transportation on the muddy roads becomes all but impossible as wheels become bogged down. Even walking becomes a laborious task as more sticky clay accumulates on one's shoes with every step.

Though they often cursed the soil, people came like revelers to Mardi Gras because of the potential it held for agriculture. The fertile land was Texas' first black gold. Long before oil was discovered in the state, creating a boom as people rushed to cash in, the prairie's rich black soil was reported to be the most fertile in country, setting in motion a Blackland boom that drew hordes of people, including many of my ancestors.

Unlike the sandy soil in eastern Texas that was easily worn out after a few years, the rich black soil had a reputation for growing things year after year. As Lamar County native son William Owens relates in his autobiography, *This Stubborn Soil*, "you can make a better living by accident on the blackland than you can by trying on sandy land."

The black soil remains fertile today because it formed from eroding limestone—cemented aggregations of millions of decayed marine organisms deposited during an earlier epoch when water lapped this far inland. Thus the Blacklands originated in the sea, and like waves on an ancient sea, the surface of the black clay soil before it was plowed was rippled with formations known as gilgai. Also called "hog-wallers" (somewhat inaccurately—they were not formed by hogs), these unusual and highly uniform patterns resemble the crests and troughs of waves on the ocean.

Gilgai formed over hundreds of years as the soils expanded and contracted in response to rainfall and drought. During rainy weather the soil expands as it becomes saturated with water. In dry weather it cracks wide open, creating deep gashes in the earth. When the rains return, water washes dirt, dead grass, and other debris into these chasms. As the ground swells once again, the added material in the soil forces the ground to heave upward nearby. Over many years, the soils are tilled up and down in a churning process that keeps them aerated and full of organic matter.

Soil scientists call soils that behave in this manner vertisols. It is a process that is ongoing and especially noticeable where the soil rests upon bedrock. As many homeowners who have cracked foundations and doors that will not shut can testify, the soil behaves like waves on the sea moving in extreme slow motion. If the soil could be filmed for a thousand years and then subjected to time lapse photography, it would indeed resemble tempest-tossed waves on the sea.

But comparisons with the sea do not end there. Because much of the topsoil in the Blackland Prairie rests atop a fortifying layer of limestone that does not allow water to seep through easily, hundreds of gallons of water per acre were trapped in the gilgai troughs. The result was a giant shallow sea punctuated with small islands that rose several inches above the surface. In fact, more than a few early observers noted that in spring following heavy rains, the prairie resembled a giant sheet of glass.

These wavy formations, in effect the soil's signature, are now restricted to a handful of native prairies and a few other lightly trampled sites that somehow managed to escape the plow. By the late nineteenth century they began to disappear, aided by John Deere's invention of the steel plow capable of turning the thick sod upside down.

The simultaneous arrival of the railroad accelerated the process by bringing about a wholesale industrial transformation of the prairies. As the dark shadows of progress stalked across the prairies in the late nineteenth century, funeral dirges for one of the world's most unique and complex ecosystems were already under way. And yet virtually no one mourned its passing; few even noticed.

By 1887–88, when Texas agricultural commissioner L. L. Foster compiled his *First Annual Report of the Agricultural Bureau of the Department of Agriculture,* slightly more than 10 percent of the prairie grass remained in many Blackland counties. In Hunt

County, only 22,121 acres of prairie remained. Already 120,484 acres were reportedly in cultivation. Another 132,950 acres were listed as pasture—which perhaps meant that cattle were being allowed to graze on sod that remained unbroken.

In Dallas County the statistics are similar: 30,120 acres were reportedly still in prairie, with 144,067 in pasture and a whopping 276,437 acres in cultivation. Telling as it is today, Foster's county-by-county report, listed matter of factly like a stock market report, was not met with the kind of alarm that greets declines in the stock market. The interpretation was quite the opposite—broken land was a sign of prosperity, of cultivation and all its attendant benefits.

Yet, as the prairie soils succumbed to the plows, a complex network of life began to unravel beneath the surface. Hidden in the soil where they were attached to the tiny hairlike plant roots, elaborate networks of mycorrhiza fungi exchanged inorganic matter—such as phosphorus and nitrogen—and water deep in the soil for carbohydrates in the plants. To the pioneers whose plows destroyed them, these delicate ribbons of fuzzy cotton candy–like fungi that crisscrossed the dark netherworld were as unknowable as the surface of the planet Venus remained until recently—hidden as it was beneath a dense layer of clouds. Their disappearance was a great vanishing act that no one saw or understood. In fact, this mass extermination of underground life was perhaps one of the key reasons the prairie would not rise again.

Scientists are just now beginning to tease apart the beneficial and often crucial role mycorrhiza fungi play in the complex prairie ecosystem. Besides providing fare for a number of creatures such as earthworms and other subterranean organisms that dine on them, their presence helps plants utilize resources in the soil, leading to improved drought tolerance and a host of other benefits. Moreover, the seeds of many prairie grasses are unable to germinate without these spores in the soil. This may be the reason why prairie grasses still exist along fences but have made few inroads into the old pastures nearby.

FIRE AND RAIN

Rains. These chiefly occur in the months of December, January, and February. At other periods of the year the rains are frequent, and particularly those resulting from electrical conditions of the atmosphere. . . . The latter months of summer are liable to a deficiency of rain, and corn and cotton planted at a late season may suffer from drought; but it does not affect crops planted at the usual time.

Edward Smith, *Account of a Journey through North-Eastern Texas Undertaken in 1849*

Let us see—Texas like every other country is divided into hilly and level land, the latter, prairies here, and they constitute the greater portions. It is perfectly flat, the soil is deep and rich; but it rains here, as well as in other parts of the world, then the prairies look like a vast sheet of water, there is no way for it to run off, and there it stands, forming many stagnant pools until the sun dries it up; When it ceases to rain, the heat of the sun parches everything, there is no shade, and great numbers of cattle perish for water on account of hot weather.

Thomas Howell, 1852

Fire played a key role in shaping the prairies as well as in maintaining them.

WHEN I was child, the Kansas City Southern railroad passed about a mile north of our house. Sometimes as I tossed in my bed at night, I would listen for a train to blow its whistle at each of the dirt road crossings it rumbled past in the darkness. Where was it going? Where had it been? A loose rail depressed repeatedly by each passing wheel drummed out a rhythmical song: *click-click, click-click . . . click-click, click-click . . .* After the train rolled on into the night and out of earshot I always felt lonely—left with nothing but silence to lull me to sleep.

Sparks flying from the passing trains often ignited the grasses, leaving a front of wildfires burning for miles and miles along the tracks. One night I remember waking to the sound of sirens and my dad hurriedly getting dressed to go and help the volunteer fire department put out a fire ignited by the train. The image of the orange glow and smoky haze on the dark horizon is still fresh in my mind. Occasionally the wildfire would ignite a tall cedar tree, sending raw flames and sparks high enough to be visible from my bedroom window a mile away. We remained up most of the night as wildfire licked its way closer and closer to our home. The fire never reached us, but it made a strong impression on my young mind.

The next morning my dad took me to see what the fire had done. What we saw was a blackened landscape with scattered tufts of grass and piles of cow manure still smoking in the morning air thick with the smell of burned grass. Blackened fence posts were everywhere, many left hanging from the strands of barbed wire stretched between them.

When I was a little older I tagged along on these adrenaline adventures, toting a wet tow sack. My job, like that of the other soldiers in the hastily mustered rag-tag army of volunteer firefighters, was to slam the sack repeatedly into the dancing flames. It did not matter when or where it happened—the fire had to be stopped.

When the fire alarm rang in Campbell, Mr. Julian, the school principal, would let some of the older boys drop everything and run the half mile to the fire station to join the men around town who manned the fire trucks. More than once, I am told, mischievous kids figured out that one could play hooky and light matches and toss them into pastures to get the others out of school to fight fires. One dry Christmas a cigarette tossed from a passing car interrupted our visit with family until the fire was put out.

During a recent summer the same type of chicanery kept firefighters all over Hunt County busy for a couple of months. As the county faced one of the worst droughts on record, pyromaniacs repeatedly and deliberately tossed matches into brown grass baked by the summer sun. Fueled by dry grass, the intense fires were more than the local fire departments could handle. U.S. Forest Service helicopters and airplanes had to be brought in to help combat the blazes that destroyed several homes and barns. As the fires raged out of control, desperate homeowners resorted to watering their yards and roofs with garden hoses to keep them from igniting. Helicopters crisscrossing the skies became a familiar sight, and we were reminded that when humans are pitted against nature, the odds are stacked squarely against us.

Fire played a key role in shaping the prairies as well as in maintaining them. American Indians inhabiting the Great Plains set fires for a number of reasons, though how extensively and for what purposes are hotly debated. Because lightning also ignited fires naturally, it is difficult to know the frequency and causes of past fires. Numerous historical accounts suggest that the Caddo Indians, who inhabited much of eastern Texas including the Blackland Prairie, used fire to flush game as well as to relieve the land of ticks and chiggers.

Other accounts, such as Pierre Marie Francois Pages's *A Journey through Texas in 1767*, reveal that Indians set fires to conceal their tracks as they fled from pursuers. A Frenchman in his early twenties, Pages was undertaking a remarkable trip around the world. Setting out from France, he made way his to New Orleans and then journeyed up the Red River, disembarking at Natchitoches in New France. The young Frenchman reached Nacogdoches in New Spain after slugging his way through dark forests and bivouacking in flooded river bottoms. The next leg of his journey took him to San Antonio on the southern tip of the Blackland Prairie, where he paused before setting out for Mexico and then across the Pacific Ocean. In San Antonio the world traveler described a wide variety of details about life in the northern tip of Spain's empire. After elaborating on the conflicts between the Spanish and the Indians, Pages revealed that "both Spaniards and Indians try to hide their trails by setting fire to the grass in the area they leave behind them, so that one often finds two or three leagues at a time burned off."

Another insightful eyewitness account of Indians using fire on the prairies comes on the eve of Prairie Time. After returning to the United States from a seventeen-year stint in Europe, where he had written *The Sketch Book* containing such famous works of literature as "The Legend of Sleepy Hollow" and "Rip Van Winkle," a man named Washington Irving set out to explore the American West. In 1832 this native New Yorker found his desire to see new places being satisfied on a rugged expedition across the prairies north of the Red River in what is today Oklahoma.

His month-long expedition in the fall of 1832, which he records in *A Tour of the Prairies*, chronicles for eternity the lost world of the Indian and the prairie. Ironically, Irving was accompanying an entourage of frontiersmen, including Henry Leavitt Ellsworth, an agent sent by the federal government to oversee the displacement of the Americans who spoke such languages as Creek, Cherokee, Choctaw, Chickasaw, and Seminole. These peoples were being forced to leave their forested ancestral lands in the southeastern United States and marched to the grassland "deserts" of the Great Plains that Anglo Americans still shunned as uninhabitable. An insightful writer, Irving painted graphic images with his pen; his impressions still stir the imagination, evoking Prairie Time. Although his explorations were all north of the Red River, the world he encountered was similar to the Blacklands farther south, and his account provides windows on a setting that knew no political boundaries.

One of Irving's particularly evocative scenes reveals the extent to which fire was utilized by the human inhabitants of the prairies and is strangely reminiscent of a recent summer in Texas when a cloudy haze from Mexican forest fires choked the sun with smoke, thick like yellow soup. Irving observed: "The weather was verging into that serene but somewhat arid season called Indian Summer. There was a smoky haze in the atmosphere that tempered the brightness of the sunshine into a golden tint, softening the features of the landscape, and giving a vagueness to the outlines of distant objects. This haziness was daily increasing and was attributed to the burning of distant prairies by the Indian hunting parties."

The sight must have inspired excitement, and perhaps even awe, among this motley crew of Anglos in an alien world.

The first wave of restless drifters who began to trickle into the Blacklands had a different reaction, making haste to rid the land of the Indians and the fires they set. Long before the first plows began to slice into the soil, severing the roots and the rhizomes that had carried the prairie across an eternity, the death of the first Americans and the ending of the fires they had ignited would set in motion a chain reaction that would leave the prairie forever altered.

Early American settlers entering the prairies from the young nation's back door were often alarmed at what they saw. The land was extremely dry in summer, and the sight of prairie fires burning across the horizon was more feared than tornadoes raging across the landscape. A tornado usually cuts a narrow swath of destruction and often lasts less than an hour. Wildfires, on the other hand, could consume thousands of acres across a front several miles wide and could burn for days or even weeks.

Ecologists once considered these fires unnatural disturbances—yet the relationship between fire and grass is certainly as normal as that between a man's face and his razor. For a time early Anglo pioneers continued the Indians' rite of spring. They watched as the orange flames swept high into the air, tracing broad arcs skyward and frolicking in the tall grass, popping like the sounds of gunfire and consuming the weathered brown blades in an instant. Once this dance of death was complete, only a blackened, charred landscape of ashes remained. For some it was a miracle, a time of newness, of rebirth, as the skeletal remains of last year's lushness were swept away. The sacrifice of the old made way for the new and gave life to the prairie in return. Ironically, before houses made of wood were in place, lighting fires on the prairie was no more irresponsible than using a tractor to combat tall weeds.

But soon the beauty of fire was forgotten. The misshapen belief that fire was bad was probably rooted in deep-seated cultural fear. An early description of wildfire in Dallas County in 1847 or 1848 written by a settler named John Billingsley is especially graphic: "The fire came in a breast a mile wide roaring like a tornado, curling, surging, and catching fifty yards away and then on again with the speed of the wind." Nothing could stop these fires as they leapt roads, rivers, and even wooded areas.

In the summer of 1860, with the Civil War looming on the horizon, tensions in North Texas were running as high as the triple-digit readings on the thermometers. North Texas was on the raw edge of the frontier and peopled with a diverse mix of emigrants—some supporters of slavery and some opposed to it. The area was troubled with violence similar to that which occurred on the prairies of Kansas as those who supported the South's peculiar institution and those who did not attacked each other in bloody combat.

That summer a series of destructive wildfires—possibly started by phosphorus matches—swept across the North Texas prairies. The flames were blamed on "radicals" seeking to abolish slavery. The ensuing panic led to an orgy of hangings meant to free the countryside of all dissent and make the state safe for the Confederacy. All across the prairies of North Texas trees were decorated with swinging bodies—a warning to Union sympathizers and a testament to the lawlessness of the slavery supporters. As historian Richard McCaslin has pointed out in *Tainted Breeze*, in 1862 the Cooke County town of Gainesville made national news when well over fifty people alleged to have been Union sympathizers were lynched.

Much of this violence was centered on the northern Blacklands as mob rule infected the parts of northeastern Texas near the headwaters of the Sulphur and Sabine rivers. In *Brush Men and Vigilantes,* the late David Pickering and Judy Falls paint a detailed picture of several Union sympathizers who were forced to hide out in the "brush" that had grown up on the prairies to avoid being tracked down and hanged. These brushy thickets made wonderful hideouts for anyone seeking to evade detection; in the years before and after the Civil War, a variety of people from Indians to outlaws as well as Unionists sought shelter in their confines.

By the time the Civil War ignited, most of the Indians who had once lived and hunted on the northern Blackland Prairie had been wiped out. As a result, the evidence suggests, the prairies were no longer burning as regularly. Stripped of the cleansing flames, large patches of prairie began to disappear under a dark canopy of cedar elm, hackberry, and bois d'arc. These dense thickets, as they were called, formed an impenetrable maze of vines, trees, and shrubs and were sometimes several miles in diameter. They made a strong impression on pioneers from that era, who gave the largest ones names. During his journey through the prairies of Northeast Texas in 1849, an Englishman named Edward Smith provided valuable insight into the transformation already taking place by that date. In his *Account of a Journey through North-Eastern Texas Undertaken in 1849,* published in London that year, he asserted that "trees spring up without being planted, if the yearly fires upon the prairie be prevented." He also provides the best evidence that these thickets were of relatively recent origin: "It is true that wood may readily be grown upon the prairies, as is seen by the daily encroachment of the wood; so that large tracts of land are now wooded which but a few years ago were open prairie."

As these thickets demonstrate, two key ingredients in the recipe for a tallgrass prairie are fire and rain—the suppression of the former was the first step toward its eventual demise. Although it takes these two to make the prairie tango, pioneer settlers prayed for one and cursed the other. Perhaps no other natural element on the prairie was so misunderstood—and so vitally important—as the flames that periodically swept away the dead material. As the fire rolled across the dry grass, it made love to the earth. Without the flames and the chemical changes they induce in the soil, many of the grasses, especially big bluestem, lose vitality and do not bloom or make seeds.

It is impossible to visit a prairie without being reminded that important pieces of the ecological puzzle are still missing. Although a small tract of unplowed prairie may still shelter many of the plants that were once widespread, other key elements, such as the Native Americans who maintained the prairie and the insects, birds, and mammals that depended on it, are gone. Each of these organisms, including the people, took sustenance from the prairie, but more important, each gave something back to the prairie that helped to sustain and to perpetuate it.

Ecologists have too often overlooked the role of Native Americans on the prairie. Although far from being children of nature—a myth that has managed to weave itself into the cultural fabric of our misunderstanding—Indians were part of the prairie ecosystem. They used the prairie, but they did not use it up, and they did not destroy it. They may in fact have had a deeper understanding of its resources and its limitations than we realize. The plants and animals were their grocery and hardware stores as well as their pharmacies.

Native Americans, for reasons including some we may never know, lit fires that burned for days, consuming thousands of acres of dead grass at a time. The flames formed a line of fire that rushed outward in all directions, marching like an army of soldiers driven by a desire to conquer the dry prairie grasses. Fanned by winds, fire roared across the prairie like a tsunami across the ocean. The grasses burned quickly, and the flames were gone in an instant, leaving in their wake small columns of gray smoke that rose from smoldering clumps of grasses across the charred landscape.

Before the heat from the fire had even begun to cool, the mechanics of regeneration were already being set in motion. Soon spring rains would bring forth a lush green carpet of tender shoots, each one arising from roots and rhizomes underground, a phoenix rising from the ashes. Fire was a part of the natural cycle on the prairie, with the ashes from the burnt grass adding essential nutrients to the soil. When fires came in late winter or early spring, the resulting blackened landscape warmed the soil by soaking up the sun's rays and giving the grasses a jump start.

More important, the fire kept in check the constant threat of onslaught by the forest. Robbed of the life-giving flames, in a matter of years the prairie would give in to the demands of the trees that were always eager to invade the prairie and that, once well established, would choke out the grasses and resist the searing heat of the flames.

Whenever possible today, the Nature Conservancy wardens use fire as a management tool on their prairies to replicate this ancient regimen and restore a missing element to the ecosystem. David Montgomery, a biology instructor at Paris Junior College, explained to me how vital fire is one afternoon in late July a few years ago as we visited Tridens Prairie near the small Lamar

County community of Brookston. Lightning had struck an electrical pole adjacent to prairie, and even though there had been no measurable rain in over a month, within a week the burned soil was already flush with a pubescent covering of delicate green grass. Lightning from summer thunderstorms surely ignited many prairie fires, teasing a fresh crop of tender grass shoots for the grazing beasts that depended on them. According to many pioneer accounts, these fresh young grass blades were particularly sought by grazing animals.

If fire made love to the prairie, impregnating the soil with essential nutrients, the rain nursed it. Annual rainfall nourishing the Blacklands varies from an average of thirty-six inches on the western edge to forty-four inches on the east. Without this water, short grasses would have dominated the Blacklands as they do in rainfall-deficient climates farther west. Rain was the key factor allowing the tallgrass vegetation that so thickly covered the Blackland Prairie. The irony is that the ample rainfall nourishing the luxuriant growth of tall grasses also made the Blackland Prairie one of the best garden spots in the world. Rain, more than any other single factor, soil included, made this one of the most farmed regions in Texas. It is also the single most important reason why this is one of the most altered habitats in the nation.

Although rainfall totals on the Blackland Prairie are generally suitable for growing crops, the occurrence of rains is often boom or bust. April and May are generally the wettest months. Tropical depressions and hurricanes sometimes bring relief from the scorching heat and penetrating drought of summer, but loans are never taken out from the bank on the strength that it might rain.

The plants that once covered the prairie were well adapted to surviving under this regime, many sending taproots deep into the earth—the roots of compassplant, for example, are said to reach depths of sixteen feet or more. To maintain a supply of water in the summer, the prairie's Anglo inhabitants used a similar strategy. Cisterns were normally dug ten feet or more into the earth and lined with bricks to serve as reservoirs of water for use during the dry summer months. Water was funneled into the cistern from the roof of a house via a guttering system.

I can now speak with authority about cisterns. Like land-mines from a forgotten war, these mostly dismissed artifacts still litter the landscape—reminders of the people who depended on the water contained within their precious walls. Today the old cisterns are filled in with trash or covered with bent scraps of sheet metal and the collected detritus of cedar elm leaves and Bermuda grass that over time becomes a rich mulch of com-posted soil. They are filled with water the color of the black widow spiders that lurk under the tin top.

In the spring and summer of 1998—the year smoke from Mexican forest fires drifted northward, clouding the skies north to Canada—we purchased a sixty-four-acre farm that adjoins the land where we now live. Those acres were owned by a woman I had never seen who lived in the next county, but my dad knew her well and spoke highly of her. He had been to meet her several times when he needed permission for this or that, and since she had always cooperated, she was a true neighbor even though she did not live close by. Our actual neighbor rented the land from her for years as a pasture for his handful of horses to graze. One year he let us cut a cedar tree from the pasture to adorn with Christmas decorations.

The land had become "growed up." The dismissive phrase is familiar to anyone who grew up on a farm, meaning that the land has been abused and neglected. In this view what it really needs are bulldozers, chemicals that kill vegetation, and some new barbed wire to commemorate the borders and make it whole again, to rid the owners of the stigma associated with having land in such a depraved condition. But its condition did not matter to a boy whose youthful imagination sprung heavy with images of covered wagons and Indians and cowboys. Even then I felt this land was mine because I knew about every thicket, about every nuance of the creek, and about the cistern . . .

In some earlier era a house had been there—with children playing in the yard, clothes flying in the breeze on the line, supper being cooked on the stove, and that cistern holding water to make it all possible. The cistern, like the prairie that once surrounded the place, has been erased from memory. Today the only other testaments to those memories—perhaps now all forgotten—are the tiny jonquils that remember when to bloom each year. Their presence is a yellow reminder of what once was, and what will become for all of us.

When I was a child I removed the sheet metal many times so that I could peer into the dark cistern; of course I was always careful to avoid the fat black spider with the red eight on its abdomen. Then I would drop rocks into the abyss and listen for the splish-splash. I could tell how much water was in there by the time it took for rock to break the silence as it penetrated the still surface. I imagined the dark hole was so deep that if I ever fell in I would never escape. It was a sobering thought, and I always feared what could happen to a boy in the darkness down there.

After the paperwork was complete, and the property was ours to pay taxes on, I knew what I had to do. I had thought about this over and over—planned every detail and previewed it in my mind a hundred times. I would get my dad's water pump and his long extension ladder, and when the water was removed I would go down into the bowels of that cistern. A mystery since childhood would be solved. I imagined finding silver coins tossed in when children made wishes or finding a gun thrown in to cover up a crime.

As water dark with the septic funk of years came gurgling out with the force of five horses sucking through the big blue hose lowered into the water, I knew the cistern was about to give up its secrets. The rocks I threw in sounded different now—making a weak thump as they struck the moist soil below. The pit was nowhere near as deep as I had imagined. Gazing in now, I saw that the hole was perhaps ten feet deep, no more. Climbing down the ladder into the darkness where the air was cooler was something of a letdown. There was nothing of significance to be seen, just dark sand that had not been seen in years. I looked up at the circle of blue sky at the top of the hole and saw tree limbs suspended from invisible trunks. I looked at the masonry—studying the handiwork, imagining the importance of these pits.

Pioneers also set about creating small pools by scraping the earth and piling the removed dirt into an earthen dam to capture the prized runoff. On the Blacklands there seems to be some confusion about the correct name for these tiny artificial reservoirs. In most of eastern Texas they are called ponds or pools, while out west on the plains they are called tanks. Perhaps in making these watering holes on the prairie the pioneers mimicked the land itself, for according to Thomas Howell the prairie in spring became a giant sheet of water.

Such is still the case on prairie remnants such as Clymer Meadow and Paul Mathews Prairie, where spring rainwater is left standing in puddles for weeks, forming dozens of amoebashaped rain pools. When the grass thickly covers the prairie, the pools may go unnoticed until a dry shoe is placed in one. Rubber boots are clearly in order.

On a bright sunny morning in mid-April, Kristin and I visited the Paul Mathews Prairie to admire the first flush of spring wildflowers, the purple locoweed and yellow prairie groundsel. We had been there only a few minutes when a large golden Labrador appeared from somewhere, deciding to befriend us, eager for the attention and affection that Kristin happily provided. The canine was in dog heaven as she jumped into the shallow puddles with all four feet.

When we left, Kristin's feet were soaked. A crack in one of my rubber boots became all too apparent as I stepped in water-filled depressions almost a foot deep, reminding me that the importance of these ephemeral wetlands should not be underestimated. Long before there were large reservoirs and small stock ponds on every property, these small wetlands provided water to a variety of plants and animals.

BUFFALO

But one occurrence is dreaded by the settler as regards his climate . . . the rude attacks of the northerly winds. These sweep over the prairies . . . at irregular intervals, but chiefly during the winter months. Their duration varies from two hours to two or three days, and an over-coat is suddenly required, when probably the settler cannot obtain one.

Edward Smith, *Account of a Journey through North-Eastern Texas Undertaken in 1849*

When the value of the buffalo's hide was discovered, his slaughter became one of those national episodes, comparable to the 'gold rush of '49.'

William Curry Holden, *Alkali Trails*, 1930

SOMETHING about the process of changing seasons—winter springing into summer before falling back into winter—has always excited me. The slow circular transformation works its way within me as it turns, as comforting as it is confounding. Each season as the weather colors the sky and the

Americans wage an eternal war against growing grass because we misunderstand the value of tall grass.

earth with its favorite tones like paint on a giant canvas, I experience familiar emotions and déjà vu. I think this must be a trait common to gardeners and birdwatchers. Awaiting the sprouting of a seed or the arrival of a fall migrant, we cast off our tired exoskeletons and emerge renewed each season. In anticipating the brown hues of fall or the colorful blooms of spring, we become participants in an ancient drama that allows us to escape from the ordinary world of everyday.

It is an escape that I relish. Normally it is a quiet satisfaction—a seasonal mood tied to a smell or the ambient light. Sometimes it is more dramatic, as when the chilling winds of the season's first blue norther thrust aside the lazy days of a prairie Indian summer. In Texas, these cold frontal boundaries, which arrive usually by October or November, are called northers. The coldest are born in the arctic and are dispersed southward to war against balmy southern breezes that originate over the warm tropical waters of the Gulf of Mexico. Before state-of-the-art technology was available to weather forecasters, the only warning was a furious cobalt-blue darkness that roared in from the north, instantly dispelling the warm humid air and dropping the temperature perhaps fifty degrees or more.

One might compare such drastic change in the weather to the assault of European culture on the flora, fauna, and people of North America, but in one profound way the analogy fails: the changes eagerly wrought by the new arrivals would soon became permanent fixtures on the landscape, erasing the world that had been. Soon the American Indians and their companions on the prairie, the buffalo, would be subducted into the bowels of the earth.

I had been teaching college students for a few years before I began to realize that more than a few are genuinely sympathetic over the mistreatment shown to the denizens of that world. In stark contrast to the conventional wisdom of traditional Western movies, where the only good Indians are all dead, the film *Dances with Wolves* offers a romantic portrayal of Indians and focuses sharply on the callousness with which American killers foolishly slaughtered the buffalo. Many students recall with horror the scene in which carcasses had been stripped of their hides and laid out to rot.

The irony is that it did not take long, once the buffalo and the Indians were annihilated, before the United States placed them into the pockets and purses of every American. Featuring an American Indian on one side and a buffalo on the other, the buffalo nickel paid numismatic homage to the lost world of the Great Plains. This popular coin was minted from 1912 until it was replaced in 1938 by images of Thomas Jefferson and his home at Monticello. The further irony is that from Monticello the scientist-president began planning the epic journey by Lewis and Clark that signaled the beginning of the end for both the buffalo and the Native American.

When Capt. Meriwether Lewis and William Clark began their slow journey up the Missouri River in 1804, there were millions of buffalo grazing on the abundance of the plains. From the prairies of Canada south to Texas, these massive beasts played a key role in the prairie ecosystem. A century later, as Orville and Wilbur Wright refined their flying machine, the great animals were gone. The gripping story is what happened in the interim—in the last wild century on the North American prairies.

It has been nearly 125 years since buffalo freely roamed the prairies of North Texas and shaped its landscape. The story of their removal is not strictly confined to the Blackland Prairies. But it is a crucial tale because these prairies were once an interconnected sea of grass. Buffalo were so critical to prairie maintenance that some have called these shaggy creatures, each weighing hundreds of pounds, the architects of the prairie. By the time the first Anglos arrived the buffalo were aided in this process by wild horses that had spread north after being introduced by the Spanish. Although other large grazers, such as antelope and elk, joined the buffalo in eating the grass, fire was the only other significant weapon in this never ending war. Without fire and large numbers of grazing animals the prairie soon ceases to be; shrubs and young trees invade, eventually choking out the grasses and replacing them with forest.

The little we know of buffalo in North Texas comes from fragmentary accounts left by early pioneers. According to the historical evidence, some think that buffalo migrated from the Great Plains south across the Red River in massive herds in mid- to late summer, probably supplementing the small resident herds that remained year-round. The impact these lumbering creatures had on the grasses must have been tremendous—but because they were nomadic in nature and there were no fences to hem them in, the long-term impact on any one spot would have been minimal.

The buffalo carnage began on the Blackland Prairie almost as soon as the first Anglos encountered the herds. Texas martyr Davy Crockett claimed to have hunted buffalo on the prairies west of Clarksville in the winter of 1835, and others had done so before him. Yet the opening salvo in the final war against buffalo on the northern Blackland Prairies came on Saturday, September 10, 1842. The blast was not fired from a gun, nor did it kill a single creature.

It was an editorial in Charles DeMorse's three-week-old newspaper, the *Northern Standard,* published in Clarksville, extolling the virginal promise of the Blackland's buffalo frontier to a wider world: "We saw, at the residence of Mr. John Robbins, in Guest's Prairie, on Wednesday last, a Buffalo Calf, which was packed into the settlement, on horse back, a short time since. It was sucking one of Mr. Robbins' cows and doing well. It was brought from the head waters of the Sabine, about 50 miles from town, where several of our citizens, have lately been hunting. Mr. Robbins informed us, that the first herd saw in that region, some three or four weeks since, numbered at least 500 heads. Such sport as the hunting of buffalo is seldom found, so near a populous country as 50 miles."

This account places buffalo near what is today Clymer Meadow—where during parts of the year, travelers on the nearby farm-to-market road heading west from Celeste may once again spot a few of these beasts that have been reintroduced on the grassy hillsides. Strong strands of electric wire contain them, and the restless urge to migrate, or even just to move on, if it still exists, is curtailed.

For many in the Republic of Texas and beyond, the *Northern Standard* was the only newspaper for miles around. When this issue hit the streets all over Texas and the eastern United States, spring rains still brought forth a riot of color that was noticed by everyone who encountered it. Imported cattle were already grazing on the abundant grass, but it was still possible to observe the somnolent silhouettes of the buffalo as they methodically chewed their cud in vast herds. Their days, however, were numbered. Their abundance notwithstanding, the buffalo had been weighed in the balance and found wanting. Soon they, like the Indians who had observed their comings and goings for millennia, would be all but exterminated.

At that time Clarksville was the northern point of entry for people coming to the young nation so recently spun off from the

Mexican government by a little army in search of freedom to worship as they pleased and to own slaves. Headstrong and full of determination, the "Texians" were struggling to plant a world of their own in this wilderness. They came in search of whatever it was that lured those perennial wanderers along the sometimes mighty Red River south into Texas. In the summer of 1842 drought had reduced the river's flow to a trickle, compromising steamboat traffic with wide sandbars. For a time riverine commerce ground to a halt—waiting, as people were forced to do, for mother nature's whims to change and for rain to raise the water level and refloat the boats. Perhaps while they waited people would sit and talk—or read. Storytelling was certainly still the pastime of choice, though as newspapers began to sprout on the frontier, even people in such isolated places were able to read about the latest happenings from around the world.

The *Northern Standard* was full of comings and goings, as well as the era's political hype, mandatory legal notices, and classified and mercantile advertising. News from Philadelphia and Washington, D.C., and even on occasion from London and Paris found its way onto the pages. Disasters and riots in faraway places were more likely to make news than local tales of woe—the paper was the cheerleader for those who wanted to settle this soil, tame it, and make it fruitful. Though set in small print, its message reached a large audience and the fabric of this foreign country was stitched into the much larger patchwork of the United States.

More than the men with guns and knives, it was the editors and the writers, armed with their pens and presses, who hammered out the weapons of words and led the literary charges that would conquer the buffalo and the Indians and would drive the wilderness further and further into oblivion.

Perhaps Hunt County pioneer William Banta had been lured by similar tales of wilderness. In December of 1847 he and some friends set out for the wild prairie grasses that remained near the headwaters of the Trinity River. Rumors were spreading that buffalo had been seen in the vicinity. Years later he told his story in a little book entitled *27 Years on the Frontier: Or Fifty Years in Texas*. A remarkable glimpse backward to that lost world on the prairies, the stories he tells are relics from Prairie Time.

By 1847, just two years after Texas was finally allowed to join the United States, the well-watered portions were "filling up" as hordes of settlers spilled into eastern Texas, carving up the prairies into private tracts and removing the openness of the landscape. The prairie was disappearing fast and soon the buffalo would be gone as well, but there were still large unclaimed tracts waiting to be claimed.

These unlocated areas, as unclaimed land was called in nineteenth century, were a lure of almost unbelievable magnetism. Two years later an Englishman named Edward Smith noted that "there are immense bodies of fine lands yet unlocated on the heads of the Brazos, Colorado, and Trinity: but they are so far beyond the settlements, that years must elapse before they can be settled by the white man." This remarkably naïve opinion was common among pioneer observers, who never imagined such a vast prairie simply being erased from existence. They also failed to realize that in the nineteenth century, as the Industrial Revolution loomed on the horizon like a dark cloud, democracy and wilderness were as incompatible as warm air and cold.

Banta's recollections encompass now-forgotten prairie pursuits, such as chasing wild Spanish mustangs that roamed the prairies. One of his most detailed accounts involves a memorable buffalo-hunting incident. The vivid imagery he used to describe the event transports us backward. Their purpose, Banta observed, was to get a "few days' rest" from the conundrums of scraping together a living. By December the yearly garden chores were over. Winter weather would be arriving soon, and it was a perfect time to get away and perhaps return with some fresh buffalo meat. It would take them five days on horseback to reach the wild prairie grass where the buffalo still roamed—a journey that was itself no picnic. They packed plenty of provisions, which included horses, feed, bedding, tents, and of course plenty of guns and ammunition.

As soon as they reached the "open prairie," as Banta called it, the group pitched their tents in a wooded area near a creek and eagerly began searching for buffalo. They had no sooner found "a herd of buffalo in sight on the high prairie" than the weather began to threaten. Banta writes that "the north wind was blowing very cold and the sky [was] beginning to get dark with angry looking clouds." They were too excited about finding buffalo, though, to worry much about the cold wind that was already biting into their faces.

While the shaggy creatures grazed contentedly on the tall grass in the distance, the anxious men scrambled on the sidelines to plan their attack. They could now smell the buffalo as the adrenaline in their bodies pumped and their hearts raced in anticipation of the kill. Summing up the situation, they decided to hunt the creatures from horseback. Each man loaded his gun and sharpened his knife. Then each selected a buffalo. A charge was ordered and they rode off together, guns blazing. "It was not long," Banta remembered, "before the herd was on the move, and a wild scene presented itself. The herd scattered in every direction. Bang, bang, in every direction could be heard."

Before the dust and smoke had cleared, three buffalo lay dead on the brown prairie grass. It was apparently at this point that the men began to feel the icy cold wind stinging their faces and tearing their eyes. As Banta relates, "it was not long before everything was still but the whistling north wind, and it was getting colder every minute."

Hurrying back to their makeshift camp with their trophies, the men realized that in the excitement one member of their party—a fellow named John Rotman—had not returned to camp. I imagine their thoughts turned quickly from excitement to fear, and perhaps to despair as the winter's early darkness set in and John did not return. After all, they were novice buffalo hunters in unfamiliar territory, and the weather was dreadful. All sorts of explanations for his absence were probably discussed as darkness descended and the onset of freezing rain and sleet made searching for him impossible. All through the sleepless night they fired their guns, hoping to attract his attention. Yet when dawn arrived there was no sign of him.

Around midnight the freezing rain cleared. The next morning dawned clear and bright but very cold. The prairie shimmered and sparkled as sunlight reflected from the ice encasing every blade of grass as far as they could see. Soon after sunrise four of the men mounted their horses and set out in search of Rotman—with only the sound of the ice exploding beneath the crunching weight of the horses' hooves to break the silence as they headed off into the prairie.

The search went on all morning, with the men regularly firing their guns to attract his attention. Finally that afternoon about ten miles from camp, they heard a familiar voice and saw John stagger into view, tired from his ordeal and hungry from having gone two days without food. After supper that night the men were treated, no doubt again and again, to John's incredible story. He told them he had become distracted chasing a buffalo for eight or ten miles before he was finally able to bring it down. If the tale seems outlandish, perhaps even unbelievable, it is consistent with that of Josiah Gregg, whose 1840 *Commerce of the Prairies* contains a similar passage. Gregg wrote that a "buffalo bull, though mortally wounded, if chased will run miles, when if left quiet, would lie down and die in a few minutes."

After killing the shaggy creature, John thought he could simply head back to camp with the others, but he had gotten "completely turned around." The cold was now more and more severe and his fingers had grown numb. In desperation, he found himself going in circles. At dark he wandered upon the freshly killed buffalo and decided to skin the animal and use the hide for warmth. He tied his horse to a tree and then labored for some time to skin the dead buffalo. Once that task was complete he stretched the hide out on the ground with the fur upward and then rolled up inside the makeshift blanket. After getting warm, he fell asleep.

The next morning he awoke to the sound of wolves feeding on the carcass of the dead buffalo—and the hide in which he had sought shelter. Struggling to move inside his cocoon, he found that the frigid temperatures had frozen the hide as solid as a rock. Unable to free himself from the stiff blanket, he lay motionless while the carnivorous creatures tore into the flesh near his face. "When they began to grit their teeth near my head," he recalled, "I fairly trembled with fear, and I could not help hollering 'suy.'" From a small hole he could see that when he spoke, "the wolves would look all around and not seeing anything, they would begin to eat on the frozen hide so close to my head I could almost feel their teeth clipping my ears."

Around midmorning the sun's warmth thawed the hide just enough to allow him wiggle from its grasp. When he emerged, he found his horse frozen to death. He was cold, hungry, and alone on the unforgiving prairie, where his inexperience at stalking the grazers of the wild prairie grass could have easily cost him his life.

This and other historical accounts suggest that by the 1840s and 1850s buffalo numbers were dwindling on the northern Blacklands as the Anglo population began to grow. Thomas Howell, writing from Clarksville on May 5, 1852, to his brother in Virginia, added almost as an afterthought: "I had almost forgot to tell you, there are buffalo where I am; they have been driven away from this part of the country. They are now, at the nearest point sixty miles off to the west." Howell continued that he intended to join one of the regular hunts pursuing these creatures.

Before the Civil War hunting buffalo had been a sport, like going fishing, but in the decade afterward it became a national crusade. Not only were they slaughtered for their hides, their bones, their tongues, and sometimes their meat; they were also massacred wholesale because every dead buffalo was one more denied to the Plains Indians who depended on the herds for food, shelter, and fuel. After annihilating the Indians became the goal of United States Indian policy, the buffalo were doomed. Ridding the countryside of these shaggy "stupid" creatures, it was preached, would also make the western lands safe for domesticity.

By the 1870s, with buffalo hides bringing $3.75 each, people eager to serve their country were coming to kill the animals by the trainload. A killer and two skinners would venture out in a wagon, one doing the shooting and two stripping the meat from the money—the former usually being left to rot. After the hides had been dried in the sun for three or four days they were shipped to market, with those of bulls, cows, and calves being sold separately.

The killing climaxed in the winter of 1877–78, when a hundred thousand buffalo were reported killed all over northern Texas and shipped to Fort Worth or the Blackland Prairie railroad towns of Dallas or Denison. Once the buffalo had been wiped out, bone collecting became the next rage as thousands of people ventured in to collect the bleached bones dotting the prairie like white sarcophagi. The bones were used for making fertilizer or carbon and sold for six to eight dollars a ton. As William Curry Holden relates in his 1930 classic *Alkali Trails,* "the prairies presented a unique sight during the 'bone boom.' Great piles of white bones could be seen scattered at irregular intervals in various directions."

By 1903 the killing had been so complete that by one account only thirty-four wild buffalo remained in the United States, with several hundred in captivity. And buffalo were not the only victims of a culture whose rituals demanded blood sacrifice. The wholesale exploitation of the buffalo that occurred in the last quarter of the nineteenth century is merely symbolic of the attitudes of a majority of Americans toward every living thing in their environment.

Even songbirds were consumed at alarming rates. The demand for delicate, feathery gems was so great that birds of all kinds were relentlessly pursued—shot and shipped east to become bite-sized morsels in fancy restaurants or decorations adorning the hats of fashionable women. The millinery trade was responsible for the slaughter untold numbers of colorful warblers, vireos, tanagers, grosbeaks, and many others. The long white plumes of Great and Snowy egrets were especially valuable, and by 1900 they too were nearly wiped out. Because the birds attained these thin filamentous feathers while they were breeding, many were shot off their nests in wanton slaughter that left the chicks to starve to death.

The Blackland Prairies contributed their share of feathers to this fashion craze, though we have no clear idea to what extent. If the records of Henry F. Peters are any indication, it is possible that considerable numbers of birds met their fate here. According to University of Mary Hardin-Baylor biology professor Stanley Casto, in research published in the *Bulletin of the Texas Ornithological Society* in 1992, Peters killed quite a number of birds that he shipped to New Orleans. Born in England in 1825, Peters moved to America and became a gunsmith. Like so many of his American cousins, he moved west, arriving in Texas in 1850. By 1870 he was living in the Fannin County seat of government at Bonham, where he ventured out onto the prairies to shoot birds to supplement his income.

We know of Peters's exploits through his correspondence with Wells Woodbridge Cooke, whose groundbreaking *Mississippi Valley Migration Study of 1884–1885* contained ornithological data from ten of the central states, including Texas. Peters apparently killed several unusual birds on the northern reaches of the Blackland Prairie, among them Scaled Quail—which has not been seen in the region since—and Mountain Bluebird, a rare winter visitor from the Rocky Mountains.

Peters's account is interesting in revealing the heavy volume of bird skins that he was shipping to New Orleans. One especially sad footnote came in the spring of 1884, when the transplanted Englishman wrote to Cooke explaining that he had shot some three hundred Bobolinks on the prairies near Bonham.

A gregarious bird of grassy fields and open spaces, the Bobolink possesses a dark beauty unlike that of any other bird in North America because it has a black breast and a white back. Likewise, the back of its head is saffron yellow, while its face is black. This pattern reverses that of all other North American birds, and it may help the Bobolink escape the penetrating vision of a steely-eyed Cooper's Hawk, always on the lookout for a meal. When the Bobolink is resting on the ground or clinging to a grassy stalk to dine on seeds, a yellow patch on the back of its head resembles a sunflower, for which it could easily be mistaken by a predator flying overhead.

Although Bobolinks still migrate regularly through the northern Blacklands, Cooke rejected the claim—suggesting instead that Peters had mistaken them for Lark Buntings (which do not migrate regularly through the region). A year earlier Cooke also castigated a reporter from Waxahachie named Dr. Thomas W. Florer, who reported these colorful blackbirds from the prairies there; Cooke said Florer was "not much of an ornithologist." Indeed, it would have been better for the Bobolinks had they not migrated this way. They are a personal favorite of mine, and I look forward to their arrival like clockwork in wheat fields near my home on April 28 every year. These musical guests fill the air with melodious song—the avian embodiment of spring, of youthful vigor on the prairies. I flinch when I imagine Peters taking aim at a flock of these handsome birds as they sang in the prairies. I flinch when I imagine an explosion of gunfire shattering the musical harmony—scattering wings and feathers and splattering blood upon the dark soil.

Captive herds of buffalo have recently been reintroduced on Clymer Meadow, not far from where DeMorse advertised them. In this experiment buffalo have been brought in from a nearby

ranch to graze selected patches of prairie grass for a short duration. As they dine on the same grasses and forbs that their wild
ancestors ate, their impact as grazers and prairie architects is being studied over time. In this way, the Nature Conservancy
hopes to use buffalo to recreate the vanished landscape.

The reintroduction of buffalo on the prairie has also added
another element missing for many years: buffalo dung. These
grayish circular patties were once a valuable source of fuel for
prairie inhabitants and fertilizer for the prairie. Every time I step
over one when I visit this prairie I wonder if this natural com-
post will add some missing microbial matter to the prairie soil
that has been missing for too long.

'Tis—oh 'tis an Eldorado!
But the traveller, travelling through it,
May not—dare not openly view it;
Never its mysteries are exposed
To the weak human eye unclosed
So wills its King, who hath forbid
The uplifting of the fringed lid
And thus the sad Soul that here passes
Beholds it but through darkened glasses

Edgar Allen Poe, "Dream-Land," 1844

DISCOVERING DREAM LAND

Modern science with all its tools and techniques for bettering humanity never got the chance to unravel the mysteries that lurked during Prairie Time. The prairies were plowed too soon. All we have today are cursory glances at its beauty left behind by those who did see it and managed to scribble a few lines on a sheet of paper. It is not much, but it is all we have of a landscape that stretched endlessly—so even these old accounts are valuable and should be safeguarded.

Today a few tiny remnants persist—each one a dream land—where the past comes alive in sudden bursts that quicken the pulse and invigorate the intellect. They are our only visual and existential links to our past—a past we have been robbed of knowing. Thus their value is immeasurable and in their hands is placed the task of carrying the torch of Prairie Time. They are like an eternal flame placed on a monument, and we must not let their fires go out. We must keep looking for these lost prairies because there are more unplowed dream lands just waiting to be discovered. But will they be found in time to be appreciated for what they are? Will they be saved before the bulldozers and plows come to scrape away the ages?

A TALE OF TWO PRAIRIES

The operation of turning over the virgin soil is a well known cause of epidemic complaints, arising from the exhalations of the gases so long confined in the new land, and now exposed to the sun's rays. It necessarily undergoes a strong evaporation, to which is attributed the intermittent fevers acknowledged to prevail at certain periods in this country.

John Barrow, *Facts Relating to North-Eastern Texas,* 1849

It was the best of times, it was the worst of times, it was the age of wisdom, it was the age of foolishness, it was the epoch of belief, it was the epoch of incredulity, it was the season of Light, it was the winter of Darkness, it was the spring of hope, it was the winter of despair.

Charles Dickens, *A Tale of Two Cities,* 1859

"I have bad news—the prairie's been plowed," explained my friend Shelly Seymour, a young film production manager who lives in Dallas. I could hear the disappointment in her voice and I knew now what she had already begun to suspect was true. When

When you learn to recognize a prairie by its plants, then you will mourn for its passing.

her grandfather passed away a few years ago the native prairie he had stewarded for years on the black land north of the Hunt County city of Commerce had been leased to a local farmer.

I met Shelly on a cold January morning while leading a bird-watching field trip to Lake Tawakoni for Dallas County Audubon Society. As we were winding up the trip, she mentioned to me that her family owned a native prairie and asked if I would like to go and have a look. That was an easy question to answer—of course I would love to go! We arranged to meet a few days later, but first she needed to have her uncle show her how to find it.

The evening before we were supposed to go, Shelly called and broke the news to me. "My uncle told him not to plow it but apparently he did," she gasped in tones that confirmed her suspicions. She and her uncle had made a harrowing trip down the slick muddy road that day to have a look and narrowly missed skidding into the ditch. As they slid past what had once been a rare unplowed remnant of Blackland Prairie they could see that it was gone.

"He probably thought he was doing us a favor," she lamented over and over. "I don't know if you still want to see it."

I agreed to go anyway. "Maybe there will something left," I thought out loud.

We met the next morning at McDonald's in Commerce, where a group of seasoned citizens were having coffee. I recognized Joe Fred Cox, a popular local historian, recently retired from teaching history at East Texas State University, which later became Texas A&M University–Commerce. I had gotten to know him a decade earlier when I taught as a graduate assistant in his department. When I introduced Shelly and explained our mission, he was full of questions.

"Who was your grandfather?" he asked. "Oh I knew John Clayton," he quickly added when Shelly answered him. "He used to be a banker in Greenville."

Although Joe Fred was not optimistic that there would be anything left of the prairie, Shelly and I piled into her black Volvo station wagon anyway and drove a few miles down a narrow farm-to-market road with no shoulders. The sun was shining and the weather was mild, but the county road leading to our destination was still too muddy for her car, so we decided to go birdwatching in an old pasture on another part of the property near the paved road. We saw only a few birds, though we walked over a mile on a grassy pasture with scattered clumps of eastern red cedars and a healthy growth of King Ranch bluestem. But a few patches of little bluestem were returning to the old field, here and there forming patches of orange beauty.

As we walked along, a few Le Conte's Sparrows sprang up at our feet before quickly darting back into the grass a few feet away. Colored with rich ochre on the face, these pale grassland sparrows are the same color as the grass and must be actively pursued to be seen well. Although these shy birds are actually quite common within the Blackland Prairie, most people never even suspect they are present. One of a dozen or so native sparrows that spend the winter in grasslands on the Great Plains, these birds have adapted to degraded grasslands, which has probably ensured their survival.

We also heard a pair of screaming Red-tailed Hawks — their aerial courtship begins in midwinter — and we watched a Northern Harrier coursing low over the fields, looking to harry prey from their grassy hiding places. Along a wooded prairie creek nearby we heard the melancholy notes of a Barred Owl, its characteristic "who cooks for you?" revealing this woodland owl's presence. A Harris's Sparrow popped up from a bois d'arc thicket.

Native to a dozen counties in the northern Blackland Prairie, this valuable and useful tree has been introduced widely elsewhere around the country, particularly on the Great Plains, where rows of the trees were planted on the periphery of farms to serve as windbreaks or living hedges. Also known as Osage orange, or hedge apple, the bois d' arc has tough yellowish orange wood. As its French name suggests—"wood of the bow"—Indians used it for their bows. Pioneers readily used it as fence posts to string barbed wire because the wood does not rot. Unlike wood that has been cut from lesser trees, it gets tougher as it ages. The bois d'arc has unusual pale green fruits that when ripe are the size of grapefruit and ooze milky sap. They ripen over the summer and fall to ground in fall, where they are eaten by a variety of birds and animals. Some ecologists speculate that they may have once provided bite-sized morsels to some large mammal that is now extinct.

Bois d'arc trees often form the centerpiece of a dense thicket of cedar elm, hackberry, locust, pecan, and other trees that have sprouted in their shadow. This cluster is usually decorated with an entanglement of vines, such as greenbriar, poison ivy, and dewberry, which form a thorny, impenetrable barrier. Fond of seeking shelter in this mad maze are the gaudy, oversized Harris's Sparrows and their companions, White-crowned Sparrows. Adorned with pink bills and black bibs, Harris's Sparrows are large, tan-colored birds that breed in the arctic regions of Canada and Alaska. They spend the winter on the southern Great Plains, where they make a living eating seeds. White-crowned Sparrows are decorated with black and white stripes that run lengthwise like a bicycle helmet. They migrate to the southern

United States from breeding grounds in the western mountains and across the endless boreal forests of North America.

But on this visit, it was not birds we had come to see. Although their presence was welcome, we could not help but feel sad as we drove back to my house. Shelly kept blaming herself for the loss of the relict prairie. "If only I had taken an interest earlier," she said again and again. "Maybe something could have been done." Her most poignant words were these: "My grandfather loved his prairie. Saving it would have been such a great way to commemorate him."

A few days later I received a telephone call from an elderly gentleman named Howard Garrett from the Rains County community of Emory. The Rains County Economic Development Board would be meeting soon and he wondered if I would speak to them about developing the birdwatching potential of nearby Lake Tawakoni and Lake Fork. I had first met this enthusiastic fellow several years before, and he had mentioned to me that his family owned a native hay meadow near the small Hopkins County community of Miller Grove. When I said I would like to visit the prairie, he quickly agreed to take me a few days later.

A trim man with a twinkle in his eye, Mr. Garrett was unloading some lumber from a trailer when my good friends David Hurt and Randy Treadway and I arrived at the farmhouse where we were to meet him. We helped him stack the rest of the lumber in the barn and then piled into the back of his pickup truck to make the short journey through a cattle pasture wet from nearly six inches of recent rainfall. Driving across a soaked pasture would be impossible on the Blackland, but the prairie soil in the east is a sandy clay loam that holds together when it is wet, easily supporting a vehicle.

As we bounced along I could feel the butterflies in my stomach from the anticipation and excitement about being allowed to see this rare bit of original Texas. Apparently no other conservationists knew this 110-acre tract still existed, and certainly none had laid eyes on it. And I was about to experience it firsthand. I was about to cross the threshold of reality and excuse myself from the modern world. I was about to take a living walk back in time.

"This land has been in the Garrett family since 1843," Mr. Garrett explained. "We always cut hay off it once a year in late June." As was a common practice among early pioneer families, a portion of the property's rich prairie grass was preserved as a hay meadow and cut only once each year. Over time most of these grassy reserves were eventually plowed, but a handful still remain—finding them is the challenge.

When the Garrett family emigrated to the eastern edge of the Blacklands and settled on a peninsula of prairie dotted by post oak mottes, Sam Houston was serving his second term as president of the Republic of Texas. The United States was still a foreign country, and the only newspaper in the northern half of the new nation was Charles DeMorse's *Northern Standard*, published more than sixty miles away in the Red River town of Clarksville. For a few more years buffalo would still forage on the rich grasses, and Greater Prairie-Chickens still danced and strutted.

"We didn't cut the meadow last year," Mr. Garrett told us as we opened the gate and went in. At that moment everything else went out of focus. All I could see was the beautiful meadow of prairie grasses dotted with small mottes of post oaks and covered with tall blades of wispy grass. Even in the brown of winter the quality of this site was beyond my ability to comprehend. Little bluestem and Silveus's dropseed were both very common, but the surprise was seeing a greater concentration of big bluestem than I had ever seen in my life. I could not believe that the giant of grasses that became so rare with the advent of Anglo settlement was abundant here.

The skeletal remains of compassplant were also abundant throughout the prairie. The plant is named for its leaves, which look like a human hand with long skinny fingers that point north and south, allowing early pioneers used it to navigate. A member of the sunflower family, it often reaches six feet tall or more and is adorned with baseball-sized yellow sunflowers that start blooming from the top of the stalk in late May and early June. A handsome plant, it has roots that tunnel deep in search of moisture. It is seldom seen away from native prairies and is a good plant to use as an indicator that land has not been plowed.

I found the dried-out remains of slender mountain mint, an aromatic perennial with thin narrow leaves and the fragrance of peppermint. David pointed toward a female Merlin of the prairie race as she dashed above an oak grove. This small falcon has a sky-blue back and winters uncommonly on the Great Plains, where it preys on birds and small mammals. A few minutes later a small yellowish sparrow flushed from our feet as we trudged across the hilltop. With our binoculars we could see its greenish face as we watched the shy bird twist and turn just above the grass before desperately diving back into its grassy sanctuary. The bird was a Henslow's Sparrow—a grassland sparrow closely related to the Le Conte's Sparrow but uncommon in Texas. Sporting an olive green face and a rusty-colored back, this bird behaves like its more common cousin. Breeding in tallgrass prairies and healthy old fields across the midwestern United States and wintering in the similar habitats in the Southeast, this sparrow has declined dramatically.

Mima mounds—those mysterious circular hills that defy understanding—were all around us. As we approached a wooded fingerlike creek that bisected the prairie, Mr. Garrett explained that he was always glad to reach this point with the baler because that meant the laborious task was almost over. When we got back to the farmhouse where he had grown up, he showed us the old steel baler that had been powered by mules. Once the hay had been cut, it was raked into piles where it was collected by the baler and compacted into bales.

David was even more impressed with the Garrett prairie than I was. "I have never seen anything like this," he said. "We have got to make sure this prairie gets protected." The following week I called Jim Eidson of the Nature Conservancy and described it to him. "You need to go see it," I offered. "Great," he said, "I'll do it." According to those who have seen it, the Garrett family prairie is probably the best Mead sedge–Silveus's dropseed prairie left in Texas. In early April I took my friend Jason Singhurst, a Texas Parks and Wildlife botanist, and Shelly Seymour to meet Mr. Garrett and to experience the first flush of spring blooms on the prairie.

The chalky yellow flowers of Mead's sedge were blooming everywhere, revealing the true abundance of the inconspicuous sedge for which this plant community is named. The grasses were just emerging. Creamy blooms of plains wild indigo, a legume found in sandy loam, and yellow sunflowers of groundsel provided some color. Hiding beneath the waves of grass were several celestial lilies, their sky blue petals just beginning to appear in the tall grass.

In the post oak woods nearby I could hear the buzzy song of a Northern Parula. A bird of wet river bottoms and swamps, this tiny blue, yellow, and orange wood warbler nests high in the tops of trees. It is famous for hollowing out a nest in hanging clumps of Spanish moss. Though this bird was probably just a migrant here, the species does nest locally along nearby wooded streams and rivers. However, since Spanish moss does not drape itself from trees in this area, I have often wondered just what it is these little feathered gems use to construct their nests.

I have told Mr. Garrett many times just how special this property is. Not only is it a living memorial to the natural history of Texas, it is also a testament to the fortitude and courage of the pioneers who were determined to carve out an existence on the frontier. These people had to work with nature in order to survive, and no matter how hard they worked, they were still at its mercy in many ways. They were dependent on the rain, the sun, and a host of other variables that were completely out of their control.

As modern culture moves further and further from the old ways, we become impoverished by being less and less dependent on our immediate environment. One result is that we are less inclined to see ourselves as partners in protecting and maintaining a healthy and balanced ecosystem. The loss of Shelly's grandfather's prairie is not just her loss. It is our loss. It is our natural heritage and without it we are all poorer. When the steel plows went into that virgin prairie, chopping up the soil, they also cut down roots and rhizomes older than our old growth forests.

It took me until early June to find the time (and the courage) to go and see what was left of her grandfather's prairie. Shelly had not given me exact directions—other than the county road where she had turned—so I was on my own. I had no idea if I could find what was left, but I planned to look carefully at the perimeters of each field for prairie plants that might have been missed by the plow. After I had driven more than a mile, looking on either side of the road into the endless fields of cotton, maize, and soybeans, I reached a T-junction with another road. Not knowing which way to go, I made a right turn and continued my search. I had not gone more than two hundred yards when I spotted a spiderwort that is common on area prairies. Because this plant is not common elsewhere, especially in fields that have been plowed for over a century, I stopped the car.

Examining the spiderwort, I noticed that it was growing beside prairie phlox—and then to my surprise I spotted the strange leaves of a young compassplant. Looking up, I realized that in fact dozens of them were growing in the road ditch along with other grasses and flowers. What I was seeing was beginning to sink in . . .

This was it. This was what was left of the lost prairie that had been plowed. Maybe, I thought to myself—not wanting to realize the truth. Taking a few steps into the sterile black field planted with soybeans, I saw hundreds of dead roots of eastern gamagrass, which look like tiny crawfish. The chopped-up remains of dead grasses were everywhere. The scene looked like a war zone. Taking a few more steps I saw another compassplant that had come up from its deep taproot but had been poisoned with herbicide to crush its ancient will to live. Yet again it had come back—the handlike leaves appearing to reach out of the ground.

I saw more poisoned prairie plants. I realized that many of them must have kept trying and trying and trying to live until they were given a dose of death from a tank of chemicals. And yet still they were struggling to fight back, even in the face of such overwhelming odds. A few had actually defied the chemicals and were putting out fresh leaves.

I was walking in a kind of shocked panic, realizing that is what happens when the prairie gets plowed. A century ago this drama was played out over and over again as one by one native meadows were chopped into pieces to make way for row crops. I thought of the Amazon rainforests experiencing the same things even as I walked.

Prairies today are so rare; it is not supposed to turn out like this, I thought. I felt as if I were witnessing a supremely tragic event, akin to watching the last Eskimo Curlew go down screaming with shot pellets in its gut. Like the prairies that were once so abundant, these handsome shorebirds were shot down by the millions as they migrated north in spring across the prairies of the Great Plains to their arctic breeding grounds. They were again shot by the millions as they migrated south in fall across the Maritime Provinces of Canada before heading out over the Atlantic Ocean to their wintering grounds on the grasslands of southern South America.

I decided to walk the perimeter of the field and see what other prairie plants were still present. A discarded bag with "Soybean Seeds" printed on one side told the whole story. Along the western boundary, which abuts the road I had taken to get here, was a dense row of trees and shrubs that were invading the field. To avoid plowing them, the field had been tilled about twenty feet from the edge, which had saved a narrow corridor of prairie. There along an overlooked edge was all that was left of this once resilient and well-adapted environment.

Eastern gamagrass and switchgrass were the most common grasses in the narrow strip, confirming that this was indeed one of the most unusual of the original prairie communities of the Blacklands. Among these grasses was a passel of flowers including azure sage, prairie petunia, and a tall wild four o'clock with purple blossoms. In the road ditch were the spindly poisoned shapes of rattlesnake master; the presence of this plant often indicates soil that has never been plowed. Its common name comes from its value to Native Americans, who made a poultice from the roots to treat snakebite.

But I had seen enough. I planned to walk back to the car and get some photographs. As I reached my car a blue pickup truck approached slowly. Not wanting to explain to inquisitive locals what I was doing (and at lost for words anyway), I quickly drove off.

A few minutes later I passed the same heavily wooded creek where Shelly and I had heard the Barred Owl a few months earlier. As I passed the bridge that spans it I could see that this wooded creek serves as a dumping ground for the things people have discarded—tires, washing machines, and household waste by the bagful. I tried not to look too closely as I rumbled over the narrow bridge.

I drove perhaps another mile before deciding to turn around and get those photographs. Perhaps the documentation would be interesting to someone, I thought. Approaching the bridge once again, I noticed the same blue pickup truck stopped in the middle of it. As the middle-aged driver moved over to let me pass, I could see that the back of his truck was full of trash.

I am at a loss for words to explain what happened next. After the downward plunge into a deep valley of despondency, in an instant my emotional roller coaster crested as I shot from despair to elation. In my rush to leave a few minutes before, I had driven right by it.

Slamming on the brakes, I jumped out of the car without bothering to shut the door or get the keys out of the ignition. I darted almost headlong into the sanctuary of prairie grasses and wildflowers that were blooming in open defiance of everything that surrounded them. I felt like Robert Ballard when he first realized that what he was viewing on his television monitors was indeed the *Titanic*. Now perhaps Shelly's grandfather would have a legacy, I thought.

It took a long time for my heart to stop beating so fast and for me to begin looking in a rational manner at what remained. It appeared that by some miracle, about five to ten acres had somehow been spared the tragedy I had just seen. I crisscrossed every corner of this small remnant, making a mental note of every plant I could find and taking an entire roll of photographs of the diverse array of blossoms. There was the tiny white prairie rose, its five petals blooming no more than six inches from the ground. There was a clump of slender mountain mint a day or two away from being ripe enough to attract butterflies and moths. There were hundreds of eastern gamagrass plants, their blooms resembling tiny pitchforks being held in place by a buried army of soldiers like those found in China. One of the most common plants was prairie petunia, its blue trumpet-shaped blooms playing hide and seek in the tall grass. I stopped to photograph an aberrant white blossom, the first I have ever seen of this species. Another surprise was finding a yellow frostweed blooming on the prairie. This member of the sunflower family has hollow stems that are uniquely winged. In winter, water that has filled the stems expands as it freezes, shattering the plant. I have seen it only in open woods and woodland edges, so I was surprised to find it here in the full sun of the prairie.

I stopped to listen to the wind that was blowing from the south—cooling me as it reached the sweat on my forehead. The sound it made through the scattered islands of trees could be mistaken for an approaching vehicle. Through the constant din of Dickcissels that were singing from every direction, I detected the hurried notes of a Bell's Vireo, which has a distinctive, inquisitive song that carries surprisingly well over the wind. To me this vireo sounds as if it is saying: *cheedle, cheedle, cheedle, chee, cheedle, cheedle, cheedle, chu?* A nondescript olive green gem, it hides its small cup-shaped nest in small thickets on the prairie. In September, after nesting duties are complete, this small bird, no larger than a pack of gum and weighing the equivalent of a few cotton balls, flies off to spend the winter along the Pacific Coast of Mexico. Bell's vireos have declined dramatically over the past century—in part due to habitat destruction and land clearing on the prairies.

I called Shelly as soon as I got home to break the good news. I was still so excited that I was almost shouting. Her response was one of stunned silence. Normally very talkative, she was struggling to find words.

It was a bittersweet day. My dismay at witnessing the plowed prairie was obviously mollified somewhat by the discovery of a small remnant. And I also felt wiser in a strange kind of way; I had crossed the threshold into a forgotten world where I was allowed to witness firsthand the screaming prairie as it went down to defeat.

THE GARDEN OF EDEN

The garden spot of the world.

David Crockett, 1834

In N.E. Texas . . . the spirits and the mind are beautifully excited by the appearance of a country having a beautifully undulating surface, agreeably diversified by woodland and prairie, and with an infinitude of little rippling rills, breaking it up into hills and valleys. The surface is every where covered with the most luxuriant vegetation. Flowers of the richest hue, and suited to every taste, adorn the prairie. . . . To my mind no country offers so much beauty and luxury, and it is probable that the poet and the painter will ere long rank there as ordinary inhabitants; and whilst Texas has an indisputable right to its title of the Italy of America, it also lays claim to the not less enviable one of the garden of the world.

Edward Smith, *Account of a Journey through North-Eastern Texas Undertaken in 1849*

From flowers that bloom barely above the ground to others ten feet or more in height, the variety of plant life within just a few feet is remarkable.

"HOW do they pronounce the name of that town?" Shelly asked as we drove home through the small blink-and-you'll-miss-it Blackland community named Jardin, north of Commerce.

"Is it the French *Jardin* or 'Jawr-din'?" she wondered out loud, explaining that in France the word means garden.

We had just left what remained of her grandfather's beautiful gardenlike prairie four miles away when we came to this small congregation of houses arranged at the junction of two country roads. There is not much here today that would remind anyone of a garden, although certainly this would have been a fitting name in Prairie Time when millions of blooming flowers stretched all the way to the horizon and beyond.

A few minutes earlier Shelly had been trying to come to some understanding of what she was seeing. We were standing in what remained of the family prairie when she pointed to a line of trees perhaps a half mile away and suddenly exclaimed, "If you squint you can almost imagine that this prairie goes all the way to those trees."

"Or beyond," I added.

Her reaction as the three of us stomped across this virginal example of unplowed prairie was proof that even when chopped into pieces, the prairie still has the power to move people. "We have got to make sure the farmer doesn't plow this," she said several times.

As we moved across the land her grandfather had sheltered from the plow for many years, we were dream-walking in Prairie Time. The surrounding world vanished, turning black on the edges as the tunnel vision of our imagination took us closer to that lost world with every step. We crushed the aromatic leaves of prairie clover and slender mountain mint, filling our nostrils with the sweet smells of the prairie. We listened to the wind rush across the grasses, singing an ancient forgotten song. We watched the eastern gamagrass twisting in the wind and we touched the rough sandpaper leaves of rosinweed.

For a moment we became people from another era, partakers of sensory experiences long dead, in which the prairie was alive and stimulating all of our senses. Though these stimuli are mostly gone, we can taste them vicariously through the recorded experiences of those who witnessed the living prairie. Like photographs of lost loved ones, their words persist, preserving through language their interpretation of long lost landscapes. The value of these old accounts simply cannot be underestimated; they alone preserve the memory of that lost world.

Pioneer accounts overflow with references to the Blackland Prairie resembling a garden. According to many of them game was abundant—including deer, turkey, waterfowl, quail, partridge (probably prairie-chickens), bear, and of course buffalo. These descriptions suggest that the prairies were deeply moving to the people who recorded them. The legendary Texas hero David "Davy" Crockett was among those impressed by the beauty and bounty of the prairies along the Red River. Historian William C. Davis notes in *Three Roads to the Alamo* that Crockett went on a buffalo hunt on the prairies west of Clarksville shortly after he arrived in northern Texas in 1835. On January 9, 1836, in his last surviving letter—written soon after trekking through the prairies of Northeast Texas looking for buffalo and only two months before being killed by Santa Anna's men in San Antonio's famous mission fortress—Crockett called this place "the garden spot of the world."

Even earlier, Henri Joutel, a member of La Salle's expedition, probably visited the eastern tip of the Blackland Prairie during his trek north toward Illinois from the Gulf of Mexico in 1685. While undertaking this arduous journey through largely uncharted territory he recorded in his journal: "There were many turkeys and other game. The scenery was very agreeable: mottes of trees from place to place, and, in locations where grass had been burned some time ago, it was beginning to green and looked like the wheat fields of France in April."

On the southern edge of the Blackland Prairie, as the Frenchman Pages approached the Spanish settlement of San Antonio in 1767, he was moved to describe the prairies that surrounded the city in this way: "That part of the country is formed of vast prairies cut by small rivers or streams some distance from each other. These are bordered by clumps of trees where many aromatic plants grow which are unknown in Europe. I believe that it is one of the prettiest areas in the world."

Particularly telling is a series of letters written by native Virginian Thomas Howell to various members of his family back home. These letters provide some especially poignant commentary on the northern reaches of the Blackland Prairie in the twilight of their existence. Writing to his brother on March 10, 1852, shortly after disembarking from the steamboat he had taken up the Red River from New Orleans, Howell gave a wonderful description of his first impressions of the prairie and the wild bounty they contained: "Small prairies are very numerous, & they are filled as well as the whole country, with great quantities of wild fowl; & game of every description. Sixteen deer were in the field near the house, late this evening and were so gentle that they might have been easily killed if the weather had been such as to permit our going out. Red River is two or three hundred yards in front of us, and a prairie not far back: as wild geese & ducks are constantly going & coming from one to another, there can be had plenty of sport in that line."

The Blackland Prairie forms a long corridor pointing north and south. It provides a perfect migratory pathway for hundreds of bird species that overwinter in warm climates from the Gulf of Mexico south to South America. Ducks and geese are especially attracted to this natural migratory corridor. During fall migration millions of geese race south in familiar V-shaped skeins as they earnestly attempt to outrun the famous blue northers that blow in from the arctic across the Great Plains. By mid-January, after loafing on the Gulf of Mexico for a couple of months, they begin their journey northward. Snow and ice still covers much of the continent, so the trip to the northern prairie potholes, the taiga lakes, and the saturated tundra where they breed is a much more leisurely affair. Howell witnessed this avian spectacle in March, 1852, as ducks and geese were heading north, stopping to feed for several weeks on the fresh grass emerging from burned or grazed prairies and taking refuge in the water of Red River. His description of the prairie as a giant sheet of glass because of the lack of runoff reveals why it provided perfect habitat for these ducks and geese. In Prairie Time, when farm ponds and reservoirs did not exist, these temporary wetlands must have been extremely important.

Although the Blackland Prairie landscape has been radically altered, the drama is still reenacted each winter and spring as millions of migratory ducks and geese heading north stop to feed en masse on the large fields of winter wheat planted by farmers. Fortuitously, this agricultural practice closely mirrors the historical ecology of the prairie. During late winter and early spring, a bird's eye view today probably looks somewhat similar to the recently burned spring prairie Joutel noticed more than three hundred years ago.

The arrival of geese in mid-January is eagerly awaited by birdwatchers because it is the first herald of spring on the northern Blackland Prairie. To watch the blizzard of white formed by undulating waves of Snow Geese as they descend to feed on the ground—rising and falling in harmonious unison and twisting and turning on stiff wings like ballet dancers caught up in a whirlwind—is to realize that winter is almost over. To hear the cold air split by the deafening sounds of thousands of geese as they honk, cackle, and laugh across the green fields by the hundreds is to witness one component that countless others before us saw, a tiny remnant of Prairie Time. That healthy populations still vault across the continent as they always have, leaving a white snowlike wash behind to fertilize the grass, is truly impressive—especially considering that some of America's most abundant birds have become extinct.

Thomas Howell had been in Texas a month and a half when he wrote a letter home to his mother in Virginia on April 24, describing a prairie near the Lamar County town of Paris. "A more magnificent view never greeted my eyes. You could form no conception of its beauty from the efforts of so feeble a pen," he wrote, adding that he would not be able to write a description that would "do justice" to the prairie.

A month later, in early June, Howell wrote to his brother describing the wildlife he had seen while camping on Pine Creek near the Red River. His letter certainly supports the idea that the prairie and the adjacent woodlands near the Red River were a Garden of Eden: "Birds of all kinds are very numerous; they are beautiful. We had a glorious little fish-fry on the first of May on Pine Creek, about six miles from here. We caught seventy odd perch and other little fish, and enjoyed ourselves a good deal in cleaning and cooking them. There were seven of us in all, no ladies of course, we stayed all day. The Paroquetes were making their harsh noises in the trees above us, occasionally we would scare wild turkey off her nest; sent the partridges helter skelter."

This letter is especially valuable for the insight it gives about the "Paroquetes." After a century or more of unlimited carnage, the Carolina Parakeet, eastern North America's only native parakeet, became extinct when the last individual died in captivity in the Cleveland Zoo in 1918. Clothed with bright green and blue feathers, and adorned with a yellow head and an orange face, these beautiful and gregarious birds were all shot to death. According to Harry Oberholser's *Bird Life of Texas,* the only known locations where these gaudy and noisy cavity nesters raised young in Texas were along the Red River, where they were last recorded in the 1880s. Howell's letter provides early evidence of their presence in abundance in the woodlands adjacent to the prairies. Yet a mere thirty years later the woods would fall silent, the birds gone, their raucous sounds echoing no more across the hillsides.

Another victim of the destructive rampage that characterized American settlement was the Passenger Pigeon. With a population of over six billion, this was once by some estimates the most common bird on earth. Slightly larger than the related Mourning Dove, iridescent Passenger Pigeons fed in the oaks adjacent to the prairies. They migrated in such numbers as to obscure the sun. During the nineteenth century, as Americans spoke of their Manifest Destiny to overspread the continent, these beautiful creatures were wiped out in a murderous frenzy. Like Carolina Parakeets, they too were shot in such stupendous numbers that it is hard to comprehend.

There is something about the word *winter* that is foreign to the word *garden*, yet the time of cold weather is also a season of abundance on the prairie. Although the garden is cloaked in subtly beautiful earth tones of brown, orange, yellow, and gray, winter is certainly a time of splendor. In Prairie Time, winter was a season of plenty for untold numbers of raptors that came to feast on small animals such as rodents and rabbits. The birds arrive today in diminished numbers on prairie remnants and old fields with enough grass to support such prey, but many Red-tailed Hawks, Great Horned Owls, American Kestrels, Northern Harriers, and Short-eared Owls managed to survive the destruction of the prairies. They are most abundant in winter, when cold weather across the Great Plains drives them south across the Red River.

A winter evening is magical on the prairie, and the best time to experience the birds of prey that still thrive in the long grass. Part of the magic is the timeless nature of a prairie sunset—the way the light slowly and imperceptibly trades places with the darkness. Though the process is as old as the tawny, grass-covered hills, it is also new and different each evening. For those keen enough to notice, it is a busy time, as the creatures of the night begin their commute from the places where they have waited out the day. Large flocks of blackbirds, in a hurry to return to roost for the night, fly over the prairie, the avian version of rush hour on a large metropolitan freeway.

There is also something urgent about evening, and the darker it gets, the more urgent it becomes. As the sun slips beneath the grasses and disappears below the mysterious horizon, the last battalions of Northern Harriers patrol low across the fields in search of a final meal. One by one they plunge into the grassy ocean and do not come up again. They have returned to the dark grassy pockets on the prairie where they will spend the night. For the harriers, night is for sleeping.

For the owls, though, with their keen sight and hearing, night is for hunting. Among the several kinds of owls that haunt the darkness on the prairie, the Short-eared Owl is a favorite of birdwatchers because it usually begins to hunt just before dark, a trait making it easier to observe. These brown and white owls are birds of open habitats, such as grasslands, marshes, and beaches. As the darkness envelops the hillside like a shroud, the owls begin to appear against the lingering glow on the horizon. Their delicate dance across the dim sky is more graceful than that of a ballet dancer. Hunting for food that scurries close to the earth through darkened tunnels of grass, owls in silhouette bob up and down like bats.

One November evening my good friend Mark Adams, at the time superintendent of the McDonald Observatory in the Davis Mountains of West Texas, visited Clymer Meadow with me to watch this ritual. Mark was on a personal quest to see how many species of birds he could manage to line up in his binoculars within the allotted one-year time frame he had imposed. The Short-eared Owl was a must-see during his visit to the Black-lands—not because it occurs only here (it is more widespread) but because the year was coming to a close and he had not yet seen one. I could tell that the suspense was killing him as we parked his rental car on the side of the county road passing beside the preserve and waited for the darkness to bring out the owls.

"Are you sure we'll see them?" he kept asking.

My response was tempered with the fear that becoming too positive about anything can jinx the whole affair. I mumbled a few words about having seen the owls a few days earlier.

While waiting, we passed the time discussing a bright star rising in the eastern sky. This object was actually Saturn and not a star at all. As we peered into our telescopes, normally used to view birds, we could see the small golden orb with its encircling rings slowly moving higher into the autumn sky, following the same path taken by the sun and the moon. In the cobalt blue darkness to the south a crescent-shaped slice of the waning moon was already halfway across the sky. Slowly a few real stars began to twinkle high overhead in the gathering darkness. As we peered into the pastel wash still visible across the western sky, suddenly the dark silhouettes of two Short-eared Owls popped into view and appeared to dance across the panoramic land-scape—against the flaming backdrop of orange and red. I could hear Mark's sigh of relief.

We watched the birds bouncing up and down across the dark gray hillsides, occasionally dropping out of sight into the grass as they pursued their mousy prey. We listened as they called out to one another, barking like dogs in the fresh evening air. The night air was growing cold, and we could feel it biting into our fingers as we clutched our binoculars. Although short sleeves were still suitable, the evening chill of late autumn was a re-minder of colder weather to come. Across the Great Plains sev-eral northers had already pushed many birds south for the win-ter. We could hear the vesper songs of several sparrows and the tiny Sedge Wrens as they whispered in the darkness. A distant meadowlark punctuated the night air and brought a sense of clo-sure to the day.

In Prairie Time many living things were certainly more com-mon than they are today, though little information was recorded about hundreds of them. To understand better how common they were before the prairie was plowed, we must tease what we can from the scraps of remaining evidence.

A poignant example involves the White-tailed Kite, a stunningly attractive bird of prey that was hunted nearly to death during the nineteenth century. Slightly larger than a kestrel, this streamlined hawk suddenly appears, a ghostly pale apparition hovering over the prairie with wings outstretched, hunting for prey. It sports dark patches on the shoulders of each wing and a dark ski mask through the eye.

Nearly extinct by the 1920s, these kites have made a strong comeback in the past several decades, and each year scattered sightings are recorded on the Blackland Prairie, though their historical status where the dark soil once supported vast grasslands is something of a mystery. The only evidence to suggest that they once nested on the Blackland comes from north of the Red River in Oklahoma, where a nest with eggs was collected during the Civil War. They were not found nesting again in that state for over 125 years; their return is likely related to a general improvement of their numbers within Texas. Today dozens of nesting birds have returned to the coastal prairies along the Gulf of Mexico, and White-tailed Kites are starting to venture inland to grasslands again.

A few years ago on a balmy day in mid-February, Kristin and I found one of these pale kites hunting over an old field of little bluestem and other grasses along bluffs of the North Sulphur River in Delta County. Apparently a mate never joined it, though it remained there for a week, often sitting in a small hackberry tree growing in an old fencerow choked with trees. We wondered if it was it looking for a mate. A few years later I found another of these sleek kites nearby, again a single bird hovering conspicuously over a grassy field. Though it is still un-clear if they bred somewhere in the area, I found a young bird later that year.

Heirs to an abundance that once defied understanding, in a vastness of grasses that once undulated over the land in hilly suc-cession, these birds and many other creatures are still struggling to regain their former glory in a fragmented world.

THE LOST PRAIRIES

So I met with no country which I deemed fit to live on till
I reached the vicinity of Sulphur Fork prairie. The prairie is
on the dividing ridge between the waters of Red River and
Sulphur Fork. . . . Here I found a prairie of rich lands—
generally a black mellow soil, well adapted to cotton
and corn.

Josiah Gregg, *Diary and Letters of Josiah Gregg,*
July 17, 1841

The extensive plains of wild meadow, termed Prairie . . .
have features differing from those of woodland. They are,
in fact, a series of long rolling unvaried ridges of waving
grass, intermixed with flowers; but in this country especially, the view is intercepted by belts of timber on the
creeks, which give these wild meadows a peculiar charm,
and elevate the feelings whilst traversing them.

John Barrow, *Facts Relating to North-Eastern*
Texas, 1849

In the prairie remnants that persist, the past comes alive in sudden bursts—
our only visual link to a past we have been robbed of knowing.

"PRAIRIE. P-R-A-I-R-I-E. This word is frequently mis-spelled, so remember that the letter *i* is silent," my third grade teacher explained as she stood at her desk calling out spelling words.

Mrs. Callan had been educated in the old school and had been teaching since the Great Depression. She told us that one of her best spellers had once lost a spelling bee because of that silent letter in the word prairie. She also explained that the word was French, which accounted for the funny spelling, and meant "meadow." This was my first introduction to the word and it fascinated me. There was something mysterious in it, and the fact that it was often misspelled made me want to remember how to spell it correctly. Yet it would be almost a generation before I would learn what a prairie really was.

Mrs. Callan never knew what an impact this story had had on me. During that formative period in my life I must have learned hundreds, thousands of words—yet there are few others I even remember learning. The year was 1976, and America was celebrating its bicentennial. Though we learned about the patriots, the Revolution, the Liberty Bell, and other national icons, the word *prairie* was never discussed again. Perhaps that is why it took me so long to find out more.

During moments at school, and at home with my mother playing her old upright piano, I often sang aloud one of my favorite songs—a patriotic hymn written by Katherine Lee Bates.

> Oh beautiful for spacious skies
> For amber waves of grain
> For purple mountain majesties
> Above the fruited plain!

The words of "My Country 'Tis of Thee" always conjured for me images of beautiful landscapes, though none of them were prairies.

By the time the words of this song were written in 1904, no other landscape from sea to shining sea had been so totally destroyed as America's tallgrass prairies. The vast vistas of rolling hills covered with oceans of grasses and colorful blooms and dotted with grazing buffalo and other mammals were gone. Although the majesty of purple mountains looming in the distance remained, the prairie had been replaced with amber fields of waving grain. It was no longer possible to respond poetically to the singular beauty that had once stopped travelers in their tracks as they witnessed it. But as Bates also suggests in the third verse of this song, the words to which most Americans do not know by heart, this conversion was nobleness, every gain from it divine. The prairies were fruitful only when they were eliminated and turned into something useful.

My first prairie experiences were on the Nature Conservancy's Clymer Meadow and Paul Mathews Prairie, both of which are in Hunt County. I was already out of college and had just met the woman who would become my wife. We were both birdwatchers, so our goal was to look at birds. At Clymer we gazed across the fence—I had not made arrangements to visit, so we stood on the outside and looked in. Even from the road, I was impressed with the prairie hillsides, covered in grass and decorated with flowers.

On a later visit to Paul Mathews Prairie, where there was no fence, I got out and walked around. I photographed the coneflowers and the Indian blankets. The early June wildflowers were putting on a nice display of color, and it resonated somewhere deep within me. Here was an out-of-the-way place that provided a natural link with the past, to a time when buffalo and Indians lived here. I had no way of knowing that these images would grow inside me until I could not get them from my thoughts. How was it that this area had somehow escaped the plow? Why did more people not care about these beautiful grasslands? Why were there no museums, no memorials to the place? How had we let them be forgotten?

It is a fitting irony that visitors to the Vietnam War Memorial in Washington, D.C., gazing upon the black wall crowded with names, see their own reflections. This national memorial, unlike others commemorating those who fought and died in previous American wars, is deeply personal. Perhaps this is because there is a little of all of us behind the neatly carved names of those who gave their lives for their country.

Since the beginning of time, wars have taken our brightest flowers and cut them down while they were still blooming. When we see their names carved into the wall, we remember them as they were in their eternal youth — smiling, talking, loving, hugging, graduating, kissing, wedding, longing, playing, dancing, parenting, struggling . . . We must console ourselves that these young men and women died for a cause greater than themselves, or their sacrifices are just too hard to bear. It is good for us to mourn, to build memorials, and as the wind passes over us, to remember. And yet in contemplating their sacrifice we are forced to see into ourselves.

So it is with the prairie. The only memorials we have to our brightest blooming flowers are the small remnants that must somehow carry on their memory. Because the great prairies have passed from the scene, they have nearly passed from our memory. The small remaining tracts have the burden of serving as our reminders of the people as well as the plants and animals that once depended on the prairie. Likewise, it is good for us to remember, to mourn and see ourselves in the sacrifice of the prairie. For it was the breadbasket that this prairie soil became that nourished and still continues to provide sustenance for our families.

It is also a fitting irony that the prairies provide a number of metaphors for ourselves. This point has been driven home to me on numerous occasions as I stalk old cemeteries, looking for hidden prairies. There on the stones are carved reminders of the brevity of life. As I slowly weave my way through the stone markers rising out of the uneven soil, I am reminded that we want to be remembered; yet as time passes and those who knew us pass on, we too go the way of last year's blooms. Perhaps this is why it is important for us to leave something behind—even if only an unmarked bois d'arc stump placed in the dirt.

I suppose cemeteries are more for the living than for the dead. They are places where we can reflect, where we can pause, and where we can consider the fragility of life. We bring flowers to the graves of our loved ones not just because this honors the memory of the dead but also because it helps us to grieve, and to mourn.

Perched on a grassy bluff overlooking the North Sulphur River—once a dark river bottom forest that slowly meandered east toward the Red River, but today a channeled ditch devoid of woods—is just such a place. It is a small quaint cemetery studded with carved stones, though I doubt there are more than a few who still remember loved ones buried here.

Several giant cedar trees keep a steady vigil, planted perhaps a century ago so that their evergreen leaves would provide a natural symbol of life eternal beyond the grave. When I first found this beautiful little cemetery several years ago it had been closely mown, and I did not realize the treasures that were hidden there. Two ornate wrought-iron fences laid out in small rectangles caught my attention; their elaborate trim a reminder of the Edwardian generation's need to be fenced in—even in death.

Today grave robbers have taken all of one fence and most of the other—including the gate. Because the beauty of these antique wrought-iron fences has been discovered by people willing to pay others to steal them, many cemeteries are being plundered surreptitiously. In the quest for a quick dollar, fences, gates, and sometimes even the tombstones themselves are taken from the dead in the darkness. I expect one day to return and find the entire fence removed.

But it is the life, not the death, that draws me to this cemetery. One unseasonably balmy January afternoon I paid a visit. As I got out of the car and opened the gate in the chain-link fence, it was evident that the grass had not been mown for several months. Amid the erect stones was a small prairie, hanging on stubbornly in the dark soil. A year or two earlier I had discovered an even larger prairie across the road from this graveyard. Although the steep hillsides were closely grazed by cattle, there was a telling mix of prairie indicator species—plants including coneflower and compassplant, the presence of which is a good sign that the prairie has not been plowed.

There, forgotten and choked out by cedars but nevertheless growing with fierce determination to survive, was a suite of prairie plants: big and little bluestem, Indiangrass, side-oats grama, compassplant, coneflower, and many others. The steep hillsides had apparently led to fears of erosion, so the site was fenced off and never plowed. Although the tromping hooves of cattle had damaged the prairie sod, leading to washouts on the slopes, and cedar and other brushy trees had invaded, the prairie was still sitting and waiting for the right conditions to bring it back to life.

With some attention and careful management, this property of twenty acres or so could be returned to beautiful prairie in a few years by removing the brushy vegetation and allowing the grass and flowers to sprout from deep roots and rhizomes sheltered underground. In a couple of years the site should be burned to restore the chemical processes that nourish many of the plants. Every time I visit I wonder how many other abused but unplowed tracts still exist, just waiting for a rest from grazing and for a good fire to tickle their bellies.

A trend in recent years within the Nature Conservancy has been to move away from acquiring smaller tracts and to focus time and resources on large-scale projects that might allow big landscapes to be restored—where buffalo can be reintroduced and fires can be allowed to manicure the grass. Yet, especially in the case of prairies, restoring the native grasses and forbs is quite expensive. To restore a site, seeds have to be gathered, often by hand, and then planted. But the fact that these processes are time-consuming and labor intensive is not the biggest problem. Healthy seeds have to be harvested from the prairie—and are therefore a scare commodity. In addition, because the prairie remnants are few and far between, making pollination between populations difficult, there is little if any gene flow between the plants. The chances are infinitesimally small that a bird, a moth, or an insect will set down in one prairie remnant before finding another. Therefore these small prairie tracts are extremely valuable in terms of both seed production and increased genetic diversity.

Currently the Nature Conservancy is using seeds harvested from Clymer Meadow in an experimental seed increase program. As Jim Eidson showed me one June afternoon, seeds from several grasses are hand picked and planted in neat rows on an old cotton field near Clymer Meadow. The strange crop is watered by a long string of garden hoses clamped together to send water to spray nozzles attached to T-posts. The idea is to increase seed production by watering these plants. The seeds are then harvested and dried and cleaned, and they are used to restore grasses on several adjacent properties, including a 150-acre field nearby that the Nature Conservancy recently purchased to restore. The intent for the future is to make these seeds available to local landowners to establish native hay meadows that are more tolerant of climatic conditions and less dependent upon costly fertilizers.

As I walked around the prairie cemetery that afternoon reading the stones and trying to read between the lines, one stone caught my attention. It marked the grave of a child who had died on January 20, 1891. It took me a few seconds to realize that what was recorded there had happened exactly 110 years and one day earlier. I thought of my own children. Then I wondered if perhaps the family had buried the little child the next day. I tried to image the scene that had occurred a century and a decade before at the place where I was standing. How had the little one died? Was there a graveside service? If so, where had the horses been tied? Was the weather warm like it was during my visit, or was there a cold norther blasting down across the prairies? I tried to imagine the mourners huddling together to escape the cold rain that could have been falling.

I thought of the black prairie soil and I thought of those who had to dig the grave with shovels. Looking out across the ground I could see the gilgai that form ripples on the earth's surface. Turning back to the stones, I noticed that no other family members were buried nearby. What had happened to them, I wondered? Had they grown disillusioned with this stubborn soil and moved on? How many other children did these anonymous parents bury elsewhere? Would anyone still alive remember these folks? Though I might be able to spend some time in a library looking for answers, these people are all but forgotten.

Yet there I stood on the crest of that hill thinking about the past. The wind was blowing, waving the stalks of big bluestem that still grow from roots well underground, nourished from the decaying matter of what was once underwater. Prairie Time was on my mind.

A few days later Kristin and I were walking in the Paul Mathews Prairie. As we crossed the small water-filled ditch serving as a threshold into this lost world, the last threads of sunlight were weaving through fast-moving gray and white clouds, highlighting the warm rufous tones of the head-high switchgrass blades as they twisted in the wind, sighing gently. Above the clouds the evening sky was cobalt blue—fading to deep purple where the sun bade farewell to the day.

As we stepped into what seemed to be a larger-than-life prairie painting, alive with color and full of drama, I felt very small. The sweeping panorama of the sky, the conflict between the coming darkness and the reluctantly dying day, and the interplay between the shadows and the light brought to mind a billion such sunsets before this one. But those sunsets were gone, forever, like the grasses that once covered millions of acres here. So it was this sunset that I admired as it moved across this small trace of native America. In truth this was why we had come, to watch the turning of the earth bring darkness to the prairie and blot out the surrounding imperfections.

As we walked deeper into the prairie we watched a gathering of Northern Harriers cruising back and forth across distant parts of the grassy hillside, attracted to the feast of mice that seek refuge and food in the tall grass. Borne on the wind, the harrier moves with the grace of prairie grass set free from its earthly bonds. As the day disappeared the sleek hovering raptors one by one turned upward before folding their wings for a final time and then vanishing into the dark hiding places where they spend the night.

As I walked and thought, more questions than answers came to mind. What was this place like when the prairie stretched forth in all directions like the low-lying clouds that reached from horizon to horizon? Who walked across this lost world once upon a time and what lost words did they use to describe the plants, the birds, and sunsets such as this?

Linguists estimate that of the approximately six thousand languages that were spoken around the world five hundred years ago, perhaps only six hundred survive and are still in use. Sadly, many have never been studied, and when they vanish we are robbed of an opportunity to learn about them. Before the Spanish, the French, and finally the English began carving up the continent, some have estimated that there were between three and five hundred or more Native American languages within what is now the United States. Only a handful of them survive—most have vanished like the voices that once laughed across the land where I now walk.

DANCING CHICKENS

Partridges exist everywhere, and were constantly running in front of our horses. The prairie hen is very abundant, and is the size of a common fowl, but much more delicious.

Edward Smith, *Account of a Journey through North-Eastern Texas Undertaken in 1849*

All this day we passed small mounds innumerable Elevated 5 or 6 feet they are generally 15 or 20 feet in diameter and rising perpindicularly. We saw this day great numbers of Prararie Hens killed several.

Anthony Glass, *Journal of an Indian Trader,* July 27, 1808

THE only memories I have of my dad's father are of a short, stoop-shouldered man in overalls who was weathered from a lifetime of farming the Blackland Prairie. Although I was only six years old when he passed away, I recall how the years had taken their toll. In the sepia portraits I have seen of him in the

Ample rainfall nourishing the luxuriant growth of tall grasses made the Blackland Prairie one of the best garden spots in the world.

summer of his life, his youthful visage is evident, his black hair stylishly combed down the middle.

Born in Tennessee in 1886, Robert L. White migrated to Northeast Texas as a young fellow in his mid teens. Like so many others from the upper South, he came looking for work on the fertile Blacklands where cotton was king. Landless and without fortune, he soon married a girl of sixteen named Amanda Milam, a great-niece of Benjamin R. Milam, who was killed in 1835 in San Antonio by a Mexican as he fought for Texian independence. Her family too had been drawn to the rich fertile soil of the Blacklands, although many years earlier. In 1860 her mother's father purchased a large chunk of prairie land near the small Hunt County community of Clinton. Family stories recall how he donated land for the growing community's first cemetery and dug its first grave into the dark black soil.

Between 1910 and 1927 my grandparents would have seven children—the last of whom was my dad. They spent a lifetime farming the Hunt County Blackland and raising children, retiring in the early 1970s. When my grandmother was in her nineties she was fond of recalling how both she and her husband had been called Bob White. She always laughed when she explained that neighbors called him "he-Bob" while she was affectionately called "she-Bob."

When I was a boy I thought the bobwhite quail were named for my grandparents. It occurred to me only much later that the birds had been given this name first, that they had been making their lonesome call for eons. Growing up in the country, where birds were all around, I quickly learned the common birds and their calls. My favorites were the *bob-white!* of the Northern Bobwhite and the *chuck-will's-widow* of the Chuck-will's-widow.

I listened for both sounds and always felt a tinge of excitement when I heard them.

Because of the association with my grandparents, I never heard the bobwhite without thinking of them, even after I took up birdwatching in college. Delivered from humid pastures on cloudy June mornings, that special sound quickened my senses. These birds were often my alarm clock, and I will never forget the first time a covey of them nearly scared me senseless. I was about eight years old and I had just gotten brave enough to wander into the pasture alone. As I approached a lone bois d'arc tree the explosion of beating wings and the roar of instant flight nearly knocked me down. That was my first visual encounter with the these birds — and all I saw was flurry of feathers flying very fast, like a fashionably blurred photograph.

Today the bobwhites are gone from our land — probably victims of the imported red fire ants that ruthlessly attack the eggs and chicks of ground-nesting birds. When Kristin and I purchased the family farm, I listened intently for the familiar calls of my youth. Though a few Chuck-will's-widows — far fewer than I remember — still sing me to sleep on moonlit nights in May, the bobwhites no longer wake me up in the morning. The land still looks the same, but something vital to the landscape is missing. Deep inside, I cannot accept that they are gone. I find myself hoping that they will somehow return; that one day the familiar *bobwhite* call will wake me up.

Originally from South America, the imported red fire ant gained a foothold on this continent after arriving in ship ballast via the port in Mobile, Alabama, while America was reeling from the Great Depression in the late 1930s. Over the next seven decades the ants swept through the southeastern United States like a plague. We first noticed them on our family farm in 1990, and in the years that followed, the bird and insect life have steadily declined. With few predators in North America the ants march on, while they eliminate many of our native ants. Though we curse them and spend millions in failed attempts at eradication, the fire ant's impact on the natural world is all too similar to that which Europeans imposed on the delicate ecology of the prairie in the nineteenth century.

Sadly, my young daughters will not grow up hearing the bobwhite's two-note onomatopoeic call. Its haunting repeated phrase will not be woven into their consciousness like the sound of rain on a spring evening or the sight of a rainbow following an afternoon thunderstorm. Because fire ants have wreaked havoc on many of the ground-nesting birds on our family farm, my daughters may never hear the sweetly whistled notes of the Eastern Meadowlark, the summer song of which prairie pioneers rendered in words that reveal something about their character: "Eat your wheat when it comes up!" The grassy landscapes that once echoed with numerous proclamations of this maxim from the tops of fence posts are now silent, stripped of lively meadowlarks.

The architecture of these mound builders becomes visible when the grass has been burned on a prairie or grassy pasture. Every few feet are scattered the earthen lodges that protrude for several inches from the surface. Most are a foot or two in diameter, though some are much larger. When the Nature Conservancy burns prairies, these ubiquitous structures are quite evident. They are often placed in a clump of grass, the blades helping to support the soil from which the tiny cavelike chambers are formed. During winter the mounds seem devoid of life, but come spring the ants reemerge from the warm well underground.

As creatures disappear one by one over time, succeeding generations soon have no knowledge or memory of them. This presents a real dilemma for parents who want to pass on a love of the natural world to their children. The older I grow, the more aware I become of how many natural experiences that fascinated me as a boy are in danger of disappearing. The truth is that if they have never seen lightning bugs, my daughters will not miss them. Still, the loss is a tragedy, and hardly anyone is taking notice. Every time an organism disappears from the landscape, part of the place is gone too, and those of us who love the place cannot help but grieve.

My grandpa's funeral was held in the small white frame First Baptist Church in the Hunt County cotton-farming community of Fairlie, just outside Commerce. As I sat on the front-row pew reserved for family, my six-year-old understanding had not prepared me for the fact that although I could see him lying in the coffin, he was not going to sit up. That was what I wanted—what I expected. I do not remember what the preacher said, but I clearly recall watching for movement, because I knew there had to have been some mistake, and he would wake up any minute.

Perhaps our longing to bring back the prairies and the creatures that stalked them is born of the same naïveté. Sadly, we cannot recall that once upon a time, when the tall grass still sang in the wind, the unbroken prairie provided refuge to a wide array of plants and animals. One of the first species to disappear was a larger cousin of the bobwhite known as the Greater Prairie-Chicken. These members of the grouse family once roamed grasslands from the eastern edge of the Great Plains to the Atlantic Ocean. As the prairies of North Texas began to disappear, these fine-tasting fowl soon followed suit—inadvertent victims of progress and a society that viewed killing wildlife as a form of religious expression. Though the birds were hunted for food, they were also slaughtered mercilessly—often shot by the wagonload. As a result they were annihilated from Texas and much of the rest of North America in just a few years. Some sources indicate that they were still common in the 1880s but were almost completely gone a generation later.

When my grandmother's family arrived in Texas, the Greater Prairie-Chicken was part of this grassy landscape. By the time my grandfather arrived in the early 1900s they were virtually gone—though there are reports that some persisted in scattered pockets for a few more years. Today five or six generations have been robbed unknowingly of the ability to witness the prairie-chicken's unique mating ritual and to hear its strange songs waft across the hillsides.

In the early spring, as dawn slowly emerged from the mist that settled low over the prairies at night, a handful of male chickens would arrive at slightly raised areas known as leks and would begin dancing to attract the attention of females in the audience. This courtship ritual called for the males to dance and strut around, bowing frequently and inflating the yellow air sacs on the sides of their heads. Apparently the females selected mates based on the talents and skills of the performers. The whole affair was very vocal, the males delivering a cacophonous, distinctly unmelodic rhapsody of aboriginal hoots and clucks sounding like tortured wailing and laughter from a haunted house. These sounds are reported to have been audible for several miles.

Today this bizarre and strangely appealing springtime ritual no longer occurs in Texas. Two tiny populations of the endangered "Attwater's" Greater Prairie-Chicken remain along the Texas coastal prairies, but these populations depend on captive breeding programs for survival. This race somehow persisted until the twenty-first century; although it seems unlikely that it will survive to see the twenty-second. Despite well-intentioned attempts by government agencies to buoy up their numbers, the birds have declined dramatically during the last couple of decades. In 1987 there were still an estimated eleven hundred prairie-chickens distributed in eight counties along the Texas coast. A census in the spring of 2000 revealed that less than fifty individuals remained. The world's entire population is now contained in only two counties. Sadly, the disappearance of the "Attwater's" Greater Prairie-Chicken in the late twentieth century along the humid coastal prairies of Texas is analogous to what occurred in North Texas to the Greater Prairie-Chicken in the late nineteenth century.

The historical record provides little information about the demise of Greater Prairie-Chickens on the Blackland Prairie, apparently because few people were literate enough to record the birds' presence or note their disappearance. Early Texas ornithologist Harry Oberholser, whose monumental *Bird Life of Texas* was completed in 1974 well after his death, laments that no attempt was made to save the North Texas population, which is estimated to have numbered half a million in 1850. Pioneer accounts recorded during the Great Depression by Hunt County historian Ethel Cassles suggest that prairie chickens were still common on the prairies of that county in 1875. Her master's thesis, "A History of Hunt County," which she completed at the University of Texas in 1932, contains some anecdotal insight into the habits of these birds of the eastern edges of the prairie— where the Blackland Prairie merges with the Post Oak Savannah. According to old-timers Cassles interviewed, prairie-chickens returned to their "strutting grounds" in spring, but in summer when the "strutting season" was over they fed on seeds of prairie grass. In fall they were attracted to post oak trees to forage on the acorns.

Along the eastern edge of the Blackland Prairie where the heavy black clay merges with sandy clay loam before finally giving way to the deep sands of forested eastern Texas, post oaks were common. Once upon a time the shoreline between the sea of grass and the wooded coastlines formed a seamless mosaic with narrow fingerlike forests following the creeks well onto the prairies and small, detached wooded mottes resembling islands sprouting from the grassy hillsides. Conversely, buried within the confines of the forest were small, irregularly shaped prairies surrounded on all sides by trees, like inland lakes. Along this zone of overlap—known to ecologists as an ecotone—there was once an abundance of both prairie and forest that must have been particularly good habitat for the chickens.

In 1808 an intrepid young man from Louisiana named Anthony Glass decided to defy the King of Spain and trade for horses with Indians living along the Red River. Departing from just north of Natchitoches on July 5, he headed north to the villages of the Alabama-Coushattas and then northwest along the Sulphur River. Following an old road though the prairies in what is now Franklin County, on July 27 he began to encounter what he described as "small mounds . . . elevated 5 or 6 feet . . . generally 15 or 20 feet in diameter." The next sentence in his journal describes seeing prairie hens, several of which he killed—almost certainly to eat.

According to Mount Vernon attorney Bill Hicks, whose family's Franklin County prairie is Texas' easternmost patch of prairie, remnants of the road taken by Glass lie on their property. Preserved as a hay meadow for generations and never plowed, this prairie is nestled on a peninsula of sandy clay loam and is surrounded by giant oaks that are nourished by an average of forty-four inches of rainfall or more annually. Glass's notes scribbled on a hot July day two centuries ago offer us valuable insight; but more remarkable by far is the fact that the landscape he witnessed is still much as he saw it—though without prairie-chickens.

The day Bill led a group of invited guests across the waves of green grass and blooming flowers, a recent June rain shower had left every leaf and blade heavy with crystal-clear drops. It was easy to imagine prairie-chickens strutting and dancing atop one of the giant mima mounds, any one of which could have been the site of an ancient lek. These circular mounds rise anywhere from two to five feet above the surrounding ground and are often up to thirty feet in diameter. Those on Hicks's prairie are especially prominent, like mima mounds on steroids, making the prairie look like a blanket tossed across a gym full of basketballs.

Theories abound about the origin of the mounds—some wildly speculative and probably all of them wrong. Some observers theorize that they were excavated in a prehistoric epoch by a giant extinct armadillo-like mammal. Others suggest that they developed along fault lines, and their formation was brought about by violent tectonic action that shook the earth, collecting topsoil and other debris into circular piles. What is known is that these pimple mounds are found in sandy clay loam—not on the true black soil for which the Blackland Prairie is named. The mounds are not unique to prairies; they also occur in nearby woodlands. But where they do occur in prairies, they increase plant diversity, often harboring an entirely different suite of plants than in the surrounding prairie.

In recent years, citizens and agencies concerned about our dwindling biodiversity have sought to intervene on nature's behalf to prevent various organisms from becoming extinct or disappearing from a local area—a process known as extirpation. Some reintroduction projects have been successful, some have not fared well, and others have been utter failures. According to Jim Eidson, the Nature Conservancy has examined the possibility of reintroducing prairie-chickens on Clymer Meadow, but the birds are highly vulnerable to predation after being displaced. The encroachment of trees presents one of the biggest problems facing attempts to reintroduce prairie-chickens, because trees provide perches for Red-tailed Hawks and Great Horned Owls, both of which prey on the chickens. Coyotes are numerous and would provide an ever-present threat to young chickens, should the birds begin hatching eggs. In a world so fragmented, polluted, and overrun with fire ants, perhaps hoping to restore prairie-chickens is indeed a lost cause. But who can fault us for longing to do so?

Sometimes now in the black darkness of the wee small hours I hear a mockingbird running up and down the treble clef way out in a distant hackberry tree. It is the time of night when it is easy to imagine that the prairie still remains. Seldom-seen slices of lunar pie hang quietly in odd unfamiliar ways in the sky. Hiding under this cloak the prairie is still intact. Buffalo still breathe and snort, their breath forming eddies of hot air rising. Tall grasses still sway and swish in the darkness, and dawn is still filled with the chorus of prairie-chickens and wild turkeys and bobwhite quail.

The hackberry tree is just outside the yard's realm, where the mown weeds give way to those that are not cut. The tree came up as a volunteer and, because of where it sprouted, was spared a good thrashing by the mower's steel blades. It is a favorite perching place for that mockingbird with a good memory and an ear for music. Sometimes I detect familiar traces of song in the mimic-thrush's repertoire. There are renditions of cardinals, of wrens, of scissor-tails, of Chuck-will's-widows, as if the mockingbird is auditioning for the part of this or that bird in the school play. And then—like the moment when a whiff of the perfume my grandmother favored elicits a wave, a torrent, of memories—then comes an exclamation from the mockingbird that startles me as I drift back to sleep: a sharp rising *bob-white!*

WIDE-LEAF FALSE ALOE

I've seen the devil of violence, and the devil of greed, and the devil of hot desire: but by all the stars! these were strong, lusty, red-eyed devils, that swayed and drove men— men I tell you. But as I stood on this hillside, I foresaw that in the blinding sunshine of that land I would become acquainted with a flabby, pretending, weak-eyed devil of a rapacious and pitiless folly.

Joseph Conrad, *Heart of Darkness*, 1902

Distracted . . . by the corruption of our times, there still survives the pristine simplicity of first-hand human knowledge of plants.

Lloyd Herbert Shinners, 1957

"STOP the truck!" I shouted to Jason Singhurst, a botanist employed by the Texas Parks and Wildlife Department, as we sped north from the small northeast Texas town of Honey Grove toward the Caddo National Grasslands near the Red

Restoring native grasses and forbs can be expensive—healthy seeds have to be gathered, often by hand, and they may be rare and widely separated on isolated prairie remnants.

River. There we planned to look for plants growing on an out-cropping of Eagle Ford shale—a yellow sedimentary rock that is fractured and brittle from years of weathering. Because the rock lies so close to the surface the thin layer of soil that lies on top was never valuable farmland—a situation that allowed the native prairie grasses and forbs to escape the plow. Although this neglected prairie remnant is being crowded out by eastern red cedars, each June the pale coneflowers, Barbara's buttons, and a host of rare wildflowers bloom as they have for millennia.

A short distance north of Honey Grove—where Davy Crockett hunted buffalo not long before he was killed—we crested a steep hill, and as we began our descent I spotted a large patch of coneflowers growing on the right-of-way. We were try-ing to outrun a dark blue rain cloud that teased us in the dis-tance, occasionally sending a splattering of tiny droplets onto our windshield, but we stopped to examine the blooming flow-ers. Easing onto the grassy shoulder, we saw at once that this was no ordinary roadside display of color. There in careless abundance was a riot of coneflowers and other prairie flowers and grasses thriving in obliviousness to the modern world around them.

Coneflowers, known to science by the genus name *Echinacea*, once covered the Great Plains, their tall stalks presiding over the prairie forbs and grasses. Today they are among the indicator species that botanists use to identify the presence of prairies that have escaped the plow. Although their taxonomy is the subject of some debate, there are twelve generally recognized species, all of which are perennials with deep rhizomatic roots and large seeds that make dispersal difficult. As the rich prairie sod yielded to steel plows beginning in the late nineteenth century, these beautiful plants were nearly wiped out—remaining only as traces of their former glory in unplowed remnants and along railroad rights-of-way, in cemeteries, and scattered here and there along fences. Because of their medicinal value, though, today several members of the genus *Echinacea* have become extremely rare due to digging in these relict populations. American Indians valued the roots, which were dried and ground into powder for their infection-fighting properties. If modern medicine has not fully embraced the folk wisdom of these Native Americans, herbalists and other home remedy enthusiasts have done so, driving up prices and putting extreme pressure on the few remaining populations.

Peering over the fence, we saw the source of the roadside prairie. On the steeply sloping hill that angled off into the distance was a slightly grazed grassland chock full of blue wild indigo, rattlesnake master, Barbara's buttons, and many more flowers, including the tiny white prairie rose. Little bluestem, eastern gamagrass, and the king of grasses—big bluestem—were all there. This was no ordinary pasture.

I took many photographs of the flowers and the landscape, in a vain attempt to capture the stunning beauty of this rare sight and save it forever. For me photographs are a way of achieving oneness with the land and a way of showing to others the beauty of natural areas. Because so much of the native vegetation has been altered so significantly elsewhere, these small patches function as living museums of our natural heritage—perhaps the only way we can truly touch our past.

We decided to eat our sack lunches in the back of Jason's pickup as we savored the moment; the rain had moved on. A few weeks later I brought Jim Eidson and Bill Carr, both employed by the Nature Conservancy, to see the sight. Without permission to enter the property, we were unable to do a thorough survey so we had to be content to study the plants from the roadside.

My next visit was several months later, in late fall, when I returned to see what the changing seasons had done to the prairie. My heart sank as I crested the hill and saw that a "for sale" sign had been posted out front. All too often, a change in ownership brings dramatic changes to the pastoral nature of the countryside. I could only fear that this prairie would soon go the way of countless others over the past century and a half—what were the chances of a buyer showing an appreciation of the truly special nature of this unique property? What would the new owners have in store for the forgotten prairie perched precariously on the side of the hill? I decided to take advantage of the situation—to pose as a prospective buyer, walk across the property, and see what other plants were still there.

I will never forget what I saw that chilly November day and the insights that I gained by witnessing a single day in the life of this prairie. As I stepped onto the brown prairie, I could see the dried skeletal remains of the flowers and grasses that only a few months earlier had blossomed with such vigor. Instead of remaining erect, though, like they do on many remnants where buffalo or other grazers have been removed, the stalks of purple coneflower, rattlesnake master, and big bluestem were shattered. The remains of the flower heads where the seeds are sheathed were torn to bits and even pounded into the soil by trodding hooves, scattering the seeds all about. Here, I thought, maybe they will take root and grow, adding more color and life to this field in coming years. Though there were no cattle on the property that day, it appeared that they had been brought in briefly sometime in late summer or early fall and allowed to graze for a short time on the rich grasses and forbs. Although the prairie was in disarray—the plants leaning, flattened, smashed—the scene was beautiful testimony to a now forgotten ecosystem.

As I walked the sloping hillside that day under the deep blue November sky and wondered what would happen to this small tract, my thoughts drifted backward in time. It was easy to imagine that the disarray of the grasses had been caused by a long-gone herd of buffalo that had had their fill and then moved on. At that moment I heard in the crisp fall air overhead the distinctive rattle of a Smith's Longspur, a small, cryptically colored sparrow. These tiny birds breed on the tundra of northern Canada and Alaska but spend the coldest months of the winter in grazed grasslands on the eastern edge of the Great Plains—primarily from eastern Kansas to northern Texas. They arrive around Thanksgiving, usually on the first really cold norther, and remain until mid-February. The color of dead grass, they blend in so well that only the most knowledgeable observers ever spot them.

Today they occur in overgrazed cattle pastures and in closely mown fields—such as airports and similarly manicured areas. Historically, though, I have often thought that this species must have relied on the buffalo for the maintenance of the short grass. As I gazed skyward I heard several small flocks of these birds in undulating flight as they moved about nervously, looking for suitable areas to seek the small seeds upon which they feed. I took a few more steps and one flushed from almost directly under my feet. That I had not noticed the bird until it flew, spurting out its jumbled notes in urgency, is an indication of how well adapted they are to this environment. The pale buff of their plumage almost perfectly matches the dun-colored dead grass.

As I got into my car to leave, I took these little vignettes with me. On the small native prairie it was easy to pretend that the changes of time had been rolled back. In my imagination buffalo were still grazing the prairie, and the ecosystems that supported them and a host of other creatures were still intact. Although I tried to interest several people in the property, I found no takers.

A few weeks later I returned to find the for sale sign gone. I was left to assume the land had been sold and soon the grasses would be buried beneath the trampling feet of goats or other domestic animals or bulldozed into oblivion. As I roamed the road ditch, I was startled by that most Texan of greetings—"Can I help you?"

This greeting is often less than welcoming, for it expresses a deep-seated fear of strangers or, as is often the case, people up to no good. Immediately on the defensive, I turned to see a tall man looking down on me from across the fence. Fumbling for words, I remember uttering my name and what I was doing. Then, finally catching my composure, I decided I probably had thirty seconds to make my case, so I launched into a crusade to educate the man about the uniqueness of his property. With all the courage I could muster I explained to him that this property appeared to be a native prairie and that it was very valuable as a conservation site.

We exchanged email details, and I agreed to put him in touch with Jason Singhurst, who I hoped could recommend contacts for the Texas Parks and Wildlife's Landowner Incentive Program. This state program provides funds for private citizens wishing to embark on habitat restoration, such as conducting controlled burns to allow fire to work its ancient magic on the soil and the grasses. Fortunately the man and his wife both seemed eager to protect this property. As the first flush of spring growth was appearing in early April, Kathy began to photograph the wildflowers when they bloomed—taking notes and trying to identify each one. In April, Jason and David Bezanson, executive director of the Natural Areas Preservation Association, visited the new landowners and made detailed notes of the plants growing there. They also discussed ways to protect the property.

My next visit was in early May, as the blue wild indigo was in full bloom. This extremely showy legume is related to the bluebonnet but taller and much darker blue, and it was once used to make blue dye. As I walked back and forth over the hillside, taking photographs and looking at the arrays of grasses and flowers, I suddenly noticed a familiar plant lurking along the fence, hiding out under the brush.

"*Manfreda!*" I shouted to no one in particular as I knelt down to get a closer look at this rare member of the agave family. I counted about twenty plants poking through the grasses and brush along the fence. Known to science as *Manfreda virginica* subspecies *lata,* it has fleshy green leaves that resemble in texture the houseplant aloe vera, hence the common name wide-leaf false aloe.

The flowers of this exotic-looking plant bloom in early June and are unquestionably the most intensely fragrant of any on the Blackland Prairie. Their fragrance is almost identical to that of Mexican tuberose, a species of *Polianthes* often used in perfumes. As the sweet scent wafted across the hillsides, I wondered just what role this odd plant with light green leaves adorned with red spots at the base had played in the lost landscape. Known from only a handful of sites in northern Texas and Oklahoma— all prairie remnants—this once widespread species is now one of the rarest plants on the Blackland Prairie. According to Jim

Eidson, attempts to germinate seeds have proven unsuccessful, leading to speculation that some now extinct pollinator once serviced the plant. If this is the case, then what we have is in a sense the botanical equivalent of a dinosaur, a creature out of its time; one more potent reminder that even though we can save a prairie site, we have lost the prairie ecosystem, probably forever.

The plant has enjoyed a rather colorful and controversial taxonomic history since it was first described to science in 1951 by Southern Methodist University botanist Lloyd H. Shinners. He termed it *Agave lata* based on specimens collected south of the Grayson County town of Sherman and elsewhere, including Oklahoma. Sadly, this population, known to scientists as the type locality, has now been wiped out. In 1966 Shinners reclassified the species, placing it instead in the genus *Polianthes*.

Oddly, although its habitat and habits are unique, according to a Cornell University doctoral dissertation published in 1975 it is not even a distinct species. Susan Verhoek-Williams, the author of this study, reclassified it yet again, placing it in the genus *Manfreda* and suggesting that it is merely a subspecies of the more widespread *Manfreda virginica*, which occurs in woods throughout the eastern United States and blooms later, in July and August. Unlike that plant's leaves, though, its leaves are finely serrated, and according to *Shinners and Mahler's Illustrated Flora of North Central Texas*, it is almost certainly a geographic entity and worthy at least of subspecific status. The authors suggest, probably wisely, that detailed taxonomic study of the Blackland Prairie populations is needed. My own observations suggest, however, that Shinners was right.

I first saw *Manfreda* the previous spring as I stumbled around on Paul Mathews Prairie. A controlled burn had been conducted in February to mimic the natural regimes, leaving the soil bare and revealing the wavy gilgai on this "hog-waller" prairie. As the grasses began to regenerate from their ancient underground roots, I made weekly trips to observe how these natural forces shape the prairie.

A plant with such wide succulent leaves easily stood out among the narrow leafy six-inch-tall shoots of eastern gamagrass and switchgrass, the dominants on this prairie remnant. One early April afternoon as a thunderstorm developed in the distance, adding drama to the scene, I came across several of these unusual plants, which reminded me of agaves. They were growing on the top of a small crest—called the micro-high— where the soil is drier and well drained. Being unfamiliar with the unusual leaves, I later described the plant to Jim Eidson.

"Sounds like *Manfreda*," he offered at once, but then added quickly, "That does *not* occur at Paul Mathews Prairie."

"Maybe it does," I suggested, offering to show him the photographs.

"Well, I'll be switched," was his reaction upon seeing my photographs. He explained that numerous botanical inventories had been conducted on the site, and somehow the plant had been overlooked. Even more incredibly, as Bill Carr and Jim would later confirm, there were not just a few of these plants— there were hundreds scattered literally all over the property. Perhaps the fire had played a role in allowing the plants to thrive so well that year though they had been overlooked in the past. At the very least the flames had swept away the taller grasses, making them more visible.

At the Nature Conservancy's Clymer Meadow prairie preserve, *Manfreda* is scattered throughout the grassy hills. Out of fear that the fragile plants might be destroyed by the trampling feet of buffalo, which have been brought in during two recent summers to graze, fences have been erected around some of the *Manfreda* plants as protection. On a recent May visit Kristin and I made some comparisons. The plants outside the fences appeared just as healthy and robust as those within the barriers. Perhaps *Manfreda* is not so fragile when given a chance. After all, it coexisted with buffalo for thousands of years; John Deere's steel plow was harder to survive.

Soon after a March burn ripped through their home on the prairie hillside at Clymer Meadow, fresh green sprouts of grass begin to appear, carpeting the earth with the first celebration of spring. Appearing out of blackened soil still muddy from a recent rain were hundreds, perhaps thousands, of tiny *Manfreda* plants, their pointed projections emerging like dunce caps. Apparently fire had been the trigger. Yet what had it triggered? Did the fire cause long dormant seeds to sprout, or had the plant simply reproduced underground? These are basic questions, but there are even more basic questions waiting to be answered.

Just what is this plant first called *Agave lata?* Is it significant that the plant occurs mostly on a special type of prairie where eastern gamagrass and switchgrass are the dominants? More mysterious, how is the plant pollinated? Is it possible that widespread spraying of DDT and other harmful chemicals on sites surrounding these native prairies has wiped out some wasp, moth, or other insect that was uniquely adapted to pollinate the species? Although we may never know the answers, every population of this plant should be studied. Perhaps something can be gleaned that will help us protect and conserve the biological diversity of the prairies that remain.

LIVING HISTORY

These prairies extend for hundreds of miles, constituting a Goshen for the settler; and since they are too extensive to admit of being partitioned by fences, they are open to the herds of any inhabitant.

Edward Smith, *Account of a Journey through North-Eastern Texas Undertaken in 1849*

The earth seemed unearthly. We are accustomed to look upon the shackled form of a conquered monster, but there—there you could look at a thing monstrous and free. It was unearthly.

Joseph Conrad, *Heart of Darkness,* 1902

THE wilderness was invigorating, observed Earnest Wallace, biographer of early Texas newspaper editor Charles DeMorse. In 1842 DeMorse settled in the small prairie town of Clarksville on the raw frontier. In *Charles DeMorse: Pioneer Statesman and Father of Texas Journalism,* Wallace quotes an editorial DeMorse

Like a geological epoch, Prairie Time encompasses the countless eons when prairie grasses held sway before they were met by the advancing crush of civilization.

wrote in the *Northern Standard* on February 7, 1852: "Striking out into the broad prairies and looking upon the face of Nature, as the Almighty constructed it—viewing elementary rights through elementary mediums . . . has a strengthening influence upon the intellect."

When DeMorse arrived on the northern terminus of the Blacklands, Prairie Time was about to come to an end. Newspaper accounts would hasten that end. Were it not for a small number of insightful people who bought land and then carefully stewarded it, we would know little about the once extensive Blackland Prairie. We would not know the timelessness of the prairie as it changed from day to day or year to year. We would not be able to leave the modern world for a few minutes and walk backward in time over soil undisturbed for millennia.

This was my goal late when I took Kristin and our three-year-old daughter, Natalie, to visit Mr. Garrett and walk across the prairie that has been in his family for five generations. I wanted them to experience the timelessness of the place, to experience Prairie Time amid the sheltering walls of the surrounding post oak mottes where no telephone poles, cellular towers, or other signs of modern civilization mar the view.

We met him late one June afternoon. Though he was exhausted from a full day of cutting hay on nearby meadows, he graciously agreed to escort us into the prairie. As sweat traced lines down his face, he traced his family history in Texas from his great great grandfather William Garrett, who first walked upon these meadows in 1843. "William came from Indiana," he explained, "and fought in the Indian Wars there." He was apparently atypical of the settlers who made the pilgrimage to Texas because he came from the north. In the spring of 1842 he loaded his wife and five children and their belongings in three wagons and began the slow trek southward. They reached Arkansas by fall, where they remained for the winter before resuming their journey the next spring. By late May the little caravan reached a grassy prairie opening in the post oaks and decided to settle down.

We know a little about the early history of this prairie and its stewardship thanks to a family history written in 1924 by Mr. Garrett's distant cousin Hurschel Garrett, who had interviewed older family members. His sixteen-page handwritten treatise, completed while still in his first year of high school, provides a peep into the lost world that greeted the earliest Anglo Texans. One example is his description of the continuing presence of Indians and the diversity of wildlife that settlers encountered: "The Indians had burned the dead grass off during the winter and the new grass was about knee high and very green and beautiful. There were Grouse Prairie Chickens, Wild Turkeys, Buffaloes, Deer in great droves there was great numbers of Bear and Panther, wild cats, wolves and many other kinds of animals that lived in this section of the county."

The land would belong to William's son James, James's son David, and David's son William, Mr. Garrett's father. As we stood there listening to him talk about the people and the history that has taken place in these very fields, it was evident how much has changed in the past century and a half. Sadly, the diversity of wildlife that stalked this prairie is history. Gone are the prairie-chickens, the Wild Turkeys, and many other birds and animals. Yet to look out across the loud stalks of compassplant reaching skyward, their yellow faces aimed toward the sun, is to revisit the past. In the imagination the strange and distant world is alive again, a beautiful thing, the memory of a lost love, a mysterious and unexplained presence.

"William was my father, but we called him Bill," he explained. "He hired the labor to help cut the meadow and paid each man in hay—six bales a day." Stretching his arms, Mr. Garrett described how as a young child he had raked cut hay into piles so that his father and the hired hands could feed it into the baler. As sunlight streaming almost sideways from the western sky cast long shadows across the grass, he lamented: "In twenty years everyone who remembers those old days will be gone. That's why it is important to me that this be preserved and not chopped up into little bitty pieces," he revealed, his voice trailing off like the shadows cast from the mima mounds.

Later Kristin and Natalie and I were alone on the prairie, walking across the ages on thick green carpet known to the early pioneers as wire grass and to botanists as Silveus's dropseed; the narrow blades resemble long hair. This grass dominates on sandy loamy soil where post oaks grow from land punctuated with mima mounds. Closer inspection revealed that little bluestem and the long tender blades of big bluestem added to the grassy mix. But this is a prairie that needs to be viewed through a wide-angle lens, viewed as small part of a lost landscape. Because there are trees here, it is a prairie that invites, that envelops. Yet it is open, not cloistered, not claustrophobic.

From a distance the almost naked stalks of compassplant rise from the green landscape, their pale yellow flowers forming disks that mimic the summer sun. June is sunflower month on the prairie—and no fewer than six different species were blooming, including a few early rough coneflowers, a type of brown-eyed Susan found on sandy prairies and in open woods. The long yellow petals grow straight up before they relax and sag into place. Rosinweed, with its thick sandpaper leaves and happy flowers, was standing at attention but was no match for the giant coneflowers with leathery leaves and six-foot-tall frames. Hiding along the wooded edges were the delicate blossoms of gravelweed crownbeard, an odd sunflower with hollow stems.

As I wandered off to take photographs I discovered that the mima mounds were home to a strange-looking legume called multi-bloom tephrosia, with large leaves that resemble a prehistoric plant fossilized in a black seam of coal. The red and white blossoms open late in the evening and close the next morning. Before they close, they turn Marilyn Monroe–lipstick red. Indians poison-tipped their arrows with the root of this unusual legume. Looking at the blossoms of one, I realized that a murder of crows was urgently announcing the stealthy presence of an owl. A few Blue Jays soon chimed in, adding their raucous screams to the mad medley. Taking a few more steps, I found a clump of wild bergamot, a pungently aromatic member of the mint family with lavender blooms that are supported by purple stems, square in cross section.

A Painted Bunting, its gaudy red, yellow, blue, and green seemingly right from a child's crayon box, slurred its notes together from a small clump of trees. A Yellow-billed Cuckoo— the infamous "rain crow" of popular wisdom—clucked a few times from the oaks, remaining hidden. Azure sage, also identified as a mint by its square stems, was blooming conspicuously, the blossoms like tiny mirrors grabbing the color of the sky to reflect it. I had seen them do this before: one afternoon as I walked through my flower garden, I noticed how the distant northern sky—usually a pale June blue—had turned the color of cobalt glass as a line of advancing thunderstorms bore down upon us. The strong afternoon sunlight filtering through the advancing clouds rendered the floral pigments of my sage a most compelling and deeply satisfying blue—quite unlike their normal pale blue.

After the jays and crows had grown silent a Great Horned Owl sailed effortlessly, and in complete silence, from one oak motte to another. I happened to glance up as its bulky brown form swept past. A few steps later I noticed a familiar plant growing erect in the shadows of an oak tree. Favorites of the butterflies in my garden, the pale lavender blooms of slender mountain mint were being visited by a couple of those winged beauties here too. Somewhere in the spreading branches of the tall oaks a Summer Tanager called: *pit-ti-tuck.* The males sport a bright red suit of clothes—and a brightly colored bill the color of Indiangrass—though they must wear the yellow garb of their mothers until they are at least a year old.

I wandered inside the darkness of the tree-lined creek on the far side of the prairie, the place Mr. Garrett had told me he was glad to reach because it meant hay baling was almost finished for the year. Descending into the ravine that shelters the dry creek, I noticed a mass of inland sea oats, their seed heads drooping like tear drops in the shade. Once across, I saw sheltered in the tall grass the light blue blooms of the delicate prairie petunias, each shaped like a tiny trumpet. A Great Crested Flycatcher darted past and landed on a dead branch just as its mate cried *creeep!* This bird had chosen a dead branch on the edge of a tree as a perch, allowing me to see his silvery gray head and breast and yellow belly.

When it was time to go, I found Kristin lying down in the green pasture and Natalie playing beside her. I placed Natalie on my shoulders, and Kristin and I walked toward the car. Closing the black metal gate, leaving another world behind, I thought of the words DeMorse had written about wilderness stimulating the mind. As we drove away I heard the sweet melody of an Eastern Meadowlark coming from a freshly cut hay meadow—encouraging me that perhaps these prairie birds will outlast the fire ants.

Driving home I kept thinking that behind every unplowed prairie is a story that needs to be told. As the Garrett family prairie illustrates, often these tales involve people who proudly chaperone the world within their care, just as their forebears did. In other cases benign neglect has worked in the prairie's favor. We are all richer for actions of either kind; untold numbers of living things inhabit intact prairies, and we are all the beneficiaries of wilderness preserves. Now more than ever, we need this sanctuary of wildness.

I am thankful to note that people are at last beginning to recognize this. Situated north of the sprawling urban metropolis of Dallas—a true Blackland Prairie town that in many ways symbolizes the wealth that could be wrought from the black gold of the prairie's soil—is a big new kid on the block. The home of recent fast-growing cities such as Plano, Frisco, and McKinney, Collin County is one of the fastest growing regions in Texas. Fortunately, unlike in other regions, the people of this county have had the foresight to recognize that preserving wilderness is essential and that the time to do it is now, while open areas remain. The Collin County Open Space Program administers a 436-acre preserve on the northeast fringe of that county. Included within this gift to future generations are an unplowed fifty-five-acre tract of Blackland Prairie and an adjacent thirty-acre restored prairie on the site of an old cotton field.

By utilizing native grass seeds harvested at Clymer Meadow five miles away, this wasteland was converted into a beautiful meadow of grasses and wildflowers. Ten years later, butterflies are again flitting around in the grassy landscape of big and little bluestem and Indiangrass, and Dickcissels sing constantly during the summer months. Visitors can stand on a high hilly ridge looking westward toward the blue horizon and imagine the quiet serenity of the open prairie. It is a place to think. It is a place to come and let the power of the land influence the intellect.

It is also a place that that continues to yield secrets long hidden. Scientists from the Heard Museum in nearby McKinney only recently discovered that buried beneath the unplowed soil was a species of crawfish unknown to science. As Jim Eidson explains, we are only now beginning to scratch the surface and look below the prairie to see what life is sheltered there.

JULIAN REVERCHON'S PRAIRIE

The soil of the most of these high prairies seems to be upon a stratum of a kind of rotten limestone from 5 to 8 feet thick, and generally from two to 8 feet of the surface. In many places the black soil extends down to the very rock; and I have observed in some of the most fertile looking fields, on the hillsides, the soil has been washed off in occasional gutters to the very rock. This rotten limestone is white, and generally in thin shelvy sheets, and too soft and brittle to be put to the purposes of building.

Josiah Gregg, *Diary and Letters of Josiah Gregg*,
July 17, 1841

The chalk hills [were] the poorest land anywhere near, hard as a rock in dry weather and lifeless chalk at best.

Shirley Seifert, *Destiny in Dallas*, 1958

The heirs to an abundance that defied understanding, in a vastness of grasses that once undulated over the land, many species are now struggling in a fragmented world.

"THE reason I like prairies? Hmmm." Becky Rader's split-second response revealed that she had thought about my question more than once.

"Have you heard of the Dixie Chicks' song 'Wide Open Spaces'?" she asked. "Where else in Dallas can you experience such wide open spaces?"

I first learned that Dallas sheltered a tallgrass dream land as David Hurt and I sped past it. We had just turned the corner from Buckner Boulevard and were heading west on Mockingbird Lane when I spotted the tall blossoms of black sampson growing on the hillside overlooking White Rock Lake. A good friend since we met in college, David now owns a nature store and birdseed business in Dallas. In college we used to drive around the dirt roads near my home looking for unusual or interesting flowers.

"Look at the *Echinacea!*" I exclaimed as we rushed past. We were in a hurry and there was no time to examine the May blossoms that decorated the hillsides in cheerful defiance of the surrounding development.

"Yeah, I know," he said, adding, "you need to talk to Becky Rader."

A prairie enthusiast and a tireless supporter of the 150 acres or so of tallgrass prairies that still ring Dallas's White Rock Lake, Becky is among the volunteers who embody the very idea of grassroots organization, helping to bring the prairie back to life after more than a century of abuse and neglect.

That such a remnant of wide open space still remains in the heart of Dallas is remarkable, because White Rock Lake is Dallas's Central Park. Situated in the middle of one of the largest urban areas in Texas, the parkland and trails that surround the lake provide recreation and relaxation each year to thousands of visitors who come to cycle, hike, jog, or roller blade; to sunbathe, explore, picnic, or play soccer; and to watch birds or feed the ducks. For many it is a place to see and be seen. It is also a place to take the family and the dogs. Though multimillion-dollar houses flank the park, its visitors are as diverse as the people in the city of Dallas itself.

Texans like to think that everything is bigger in Texas, a boastful spirit evident in the nickname Dallas residents have given their city—Big D. "The business of Dallas is business," goes the local slogan. It had to be that way if the city John Neely Bryan founded on the banks of the narrow, winding, and wooded river known as the Trinity was to pull itself up by its bootstraps. Without the blessings of a deep river or an ocean that could link it to the outside world, Dallas might have been destined to remain on the fringes of societal evolution.

All Dallas had going for it was a huge seam of white rock that surfaced in broken sheets and crumbled easily but was too rocky to plow. It was not the rock itself that proved so valuable to business but what happened to that pallid limestone as it eroded and mixed with soil formed by the decaying prairie plants that grew a few inches above it. As it wore down over the ages it underwent a strange transformation: the ivory rock morphed into an ebony soil with almost magical powers to grow cotton—year after year.

The power and potential of the black soil remained largely untapped until after Americans worked out their sectional differences in the Civil War. Following that murderous episode they turned their energies to building railroads, particularly in the South. Between 1865 and 1900 the network of steel rails had nearly stitched the entire country into a single economic blanket that linked producers and consumers. With the help of steel—both John Deere's steel plow and Andrew Carnegie's steel rails—Dallas was uniquely situated to exploit the prairie's resources. The age of steam met the age of steel, and together these two products of the Industrial Revolution set about transforming the Blackland Prairie.

Perhaps more than any of the other Blackland towns that sprouted along the rails, Dallas fed on the farm wealth generated from the surrounding hinterlands, in the process turning dirt into dollars. It was no miracle, just the product of the American belief in a birthright to transform the landscape to fit people's needs using human strength and industrial might. And what a transformation it was. After the railroad tycoons connected the Blackland Prairie with the rest of the nation, all but a few traces of Prairie Time were eliminated within a few years.

In Dallas and the small towns that surrounded it—and would eventually be consumed by it—the transformation began in 1872 when the Houston and Texas Central railroad finally connected this fledgling city with the Gulf of Mexico. This enterprise provided the viable link to the sea that Dallas had been craving. The city had even gone as far as offering a fifteen-thousand-dollar reward to the first boat captain to navigate up the narrow and shallow Trinity River. In 1868 James McGarvey collected the prize money for navigating the *Job Boat No. 1* from Galveston to Dallas—but it took him more than a year to complete the trip.

To toast the arrival of the steel river and their independence from the fickle and undependable Trinity, the excited Dallasites, including an aged John Neely Bryan, threw a huge party on July 16, 1872, in which the celebrants dined on the vanishing plenty of the prairies. According to Dallas historian A. C. Greene, the party goers that day included Dallas's early pioneers and its modern, forward-thinking folk, and they dined on what had once been prime prairie fare: barbecued prairie-chicken and buffalo. They could have chosen no more vitally symbolic victuals than those two staples of the prairie wilderness. It was a celebration toasting the end of Prairie Time, toasting the dawning of a new era, toasting the world they were about to re-create.

The railroad party was a symbolic end to a process that had begun on the Blacklands just a short distance from the Red River at Clarksville in 1842, when Charles DeMorse began publishing his newspaper that cajoled Americans to come and feast on the fat of the prairies. The feast that hot July day was the prairie's last supper; the official closing of Prairie Time on Texas' Blackland Prairie. Of course, there would be no funeral pyre, no eternal fire to commemorate the lost world.

Now Dallas would look to a brighter future. The past was to be forgotten. The arrival of the railroad would allow cotton and other products to be shipped to market. The railroad touched off a building boom and an immigration boom that would leave the countryside forever altered. Shortly thereafter the line was extended north to Denison, where it was linked with the Missouri, Kansas and Texas—called the Katy—that came from St. Louis. Goods began to flow from the factories of the East to the growing hordes who came to farm, buy, sell, and trade, and farm products could go anywhere; the market economy had arrived.

But the underlying engine that powered the success of Dallas was not the steel rail, nor was it the steel plow—it was the soil that eroded from that seam of white rock. The ancient graves of millions of microscopic organisms fertilized the black soil and grew some of the best prairie grasses anyone had ever seen. In just a few years Dallas became the largest city in the state.

At the turn of the twentieth century, the prairie-clad hills overlooking White Rock Creek were still isolated from the developing din of Dallas's urban hustle and bustle. While people came who sought to master the rattlesnakes that had once slipped through Dallas streets, the odd-looking plant called rattlesnake master still clung to the soil near the sleepy little town of Reinhardt on the eastern side of the creek. It was a different world out there in the country. Rolling hillsides still rose above the broad flat river bottom, and cattle grazed the grass because in some places above the creek early settlers found exposed rock jutting from the ground, and what passed for soil was too shallow and too rocky to plow.

For none was this lesson illustrated more graphically than for a group of some three hundred starry-eyed dreamers who arrived in 1855, hoping to transform the white rock hills into an agricultural utopia where everyone would be equally endowed with work and profits. Calling themselves La Compagnie Franco-Texienne, or La Reunion, they came from France, Belgium, and Switzerland because they had heard Texas was a land of milk and honey. They could not have chosen a more inappropriate location. The hard rock that popped out of the prairie was hardly the place to plant a pastoral paradise. They were soon defeated, like others who tried such schemes, doomed by a unique conspiracy of grasshoppers and a freak occurrence of freezing weather in May—but mostly by that darned white rock too tough to plow.

Although this gaggle of communal free-thinkers certainly cast a peculiar shadow as they waltzed into town wearing wooden shoes, some on foot and others in oxcarts, their arrival in 1855 doubled the city's population in one instant. Radical ideas notwithstanding, it was not what they stood for so much as what they brought that changed Dallas. They came with tools and trades and big ideas that drifting Arkansans and Tennesseans lacked. In the caravan were tailors, shoemakers, jewelers, hat makers, musicians, artists, poets, and naturalists. They were Europeans with a knack for the urbane. Although they soon gave up on the stony soil, eventually the tenacious ones who remained would turn Dallas into a enclave of culture that would stand out like beacon from the modest surrounding towns of Cedar Springs, Trinity City, and later Mesquite and Grand Prairie.

They were led by one Victor Considerant, a follower of the French political thinker Fourier. Not unlike other refuges from European oppression, including the Puritans of Massachusetts Bay over two centuries earlier, Considerant and his settlers had planned to plant the seeds of a communal city on a hill in America. What they provided Dallas, though, was a quick infusion of intellectual capital unprecedented on the Blacklands of Texas. One of their number, Ben Lang, later became mayor of Dallas. Others contributed in many ways toward making Dallas an international city on the western fringe of the Deep South.

There was also a talented young botanist from France named Julian Reverchon, who had been born halfway around the world a year after Sam Houston and his fellow Texans captured Santa Anna at San Jacinto. When Julian and his father arrived in Dallas in 1856 planning to join the experiment, they found that the venture had already gone belly up, so they bought some land and settled down.

Soon the French-born botanist began stalking into the white rock hills and farther afield with the quiet obsession of one who has come to love plants. A genuine celebrity among those inclined to care about the secret who, what, when, and where in the world of plants, Reverchon cast his intellectual net widely. He collected thousands of plants, communicated with noted Harvard University botanist Asa Gray, and later became a professor at Dallas's Baylor University College of Medicine and Pharmacy. A man well ahead of his time, he planted local flowers in his botanical gardens long before twentieth-century growers began to preach that native plants are better adapted to the extremes of North Texas weather.

Dallasites have largely forgotten this early star of their city, though a city park and several plants carry his name. Appropriately enough, one of these plants grows straight out of small cracks in the white rocks he stalked. I have in my garden a tiny perennial mint with lavender flowers that botanists call *Hedeoma reverchonii*. Reverchon sent the woody perennial to Asa Gray, who named it in his honor. It is a fitting plant to have named for him because it clings stubbornly to the hard rock where other plants would wither and die.

To others who came later, it was clear that instead of slicing plows into the ground, it would be better to use the grass on the hills around the city to fatten livestock, especially dairy cows. The pastoral scenes were not destined to last, however, because Dallas continued to grow, spreading outward in leaps and bounds without any coordinated planning and overtaking the small surrounding communities of Cedar Springs, Reinhardt, Scyene, and Lisbon. Had it not been for the seam of white rock that defeated the little colony of utopians, even this small sliver of natural heritage would have been erased.

A terrible drought—the plague of the prairies—in the first decade of the twentieth century highlighted Dallas's urgent need for a dependable source of drinking water. For the city's Progressives, a unique marriage of business leaders and social reformers who believed that the efficient use of technology could solve any problem, the answer was to build a massive dam on White Rock Creek northeast of the city. If the city needed water, a dam could be built. If the city needed to grow, roads could be built. These were tenets that no one questioned. Dallas had to grow because business demanded it.

Construction of the earthen works that would serve as a dam for the creek began in 1909. It was completed two years later, and by 1914 the lake was full of water and ready to be used by the city. Soon the prairie hills that had once harbored a sea of grasses were hosting a sea of people. The result was that the ancient grasses that had been nourished for eons by organisms once on the bed of an ancient undersea world were kept cropped by mowers pulled behind tractors.

For decades the prairie languished, buried beneath a cultural stigma against tall grass. This was the situation until Becky and others who love the lake and our natural heritage decided to become involved. Becky lives nearby and hated to see the coneflowers, yuccas, fire wheels, and other prairie blossoms shredded while they were still blooming. She began making phone calls to the Dallas Parks Department, offering to help educate city officials about better ways to manage and protect this priceless resource.

"They were mowing the grasses and wildflowers in early June before they had a chance to set seed," she explained to me. "It was just the wrong time of year. What we suggested was waiting until the first week in July, when most of the plants have gone to seed. Overall the city has been very supportive and so have the various neighborhood associations."

She went on to note that when park managers started letting the tall grass grow, people began calling the parks department, asking them to mow the grass. Her strategy, which she described to me as we walked across her favorite urban wide open space one June afternoon, is to educate people. "We had to let them know the importance of what we really had here."

A lush carpet of little bluestem rose from ancient roots and almost tickled the butterflies as they sailed past. We were in a prairie, in an urban dream land surrounded by homes and Saint Augustine lawns, where flowers from every almost every continent grow in the rich black soil. Entwined and entangled about the grasses, we saw an unusual stringy growth called dodder that is about the thickness of spaghetti. This strange bright orange parasite sucks nutrients from the prairie plants as it winds around the prairie like a child's scribbles on a sheet of paper. We admired the yellow sunflowers of Engelmann's cutleaf daisy and found, buried in the grass, the pale yellow flowers of a ground cherry, a shy plant on which the blossoms face the ground. According to Euell Gibbons, this edible plant is quite tasty.

The sun was busy making preparations for its hasty departure, and rush hour traffic was beginning to subside as we piled into our vehicles to leave. While we had spent a couple of free hours in prairie dream land, thousands of people were fighting the traffic, crawling at the pace of snails, struggling to get home. I do not suppose any of them were wearing wooden shoes or riding oxcarts, although that outdated mode of transportation might have been faster for some of them.

Often historical truth is stranger than fiction—in this case a wayfaring stranger. Truth is always more compelling than society's imagined shibboleths. Dallas is more than longhorns and ten-gallon hats. It is also a quiet plant lover stalking the prairies, a man who came as a wayfaring stranger to these rocky hillsides. Visiting the hills around White Rock Lake, one of the few remnants of prairie virginity left in Dallas, it is hard not to think of Julian Reverchon—whose concern for the plight of humankind led him to a Blackland paradise lost and then found.

WHERE THE
PAVEMENT ENDS

Woe unto them that join house to house, that lay field to field, till there be no place, that they may be placed alone in the midst of the earth.

Isaiah 5:8

McKinney was founded but a year or two ago, and it small. Dallas is a rising town, well situated for commerce, on a tongue of land on the very banks of the Trinity.

Edward Smith, *Account of a Journey through North-Eastern Texas Undertaken in 1849*

"WE have a prairie cemetery you might be interested in seeing," Dallas neurologist Bill Woodfin told me one May day as we talked in the parking lot of Parkhill Prairie in Collin County. I had just met him and his wife, Fran, who raises Morgan horses. We had all accompanied Jim Eidson on a field trip to admire the native prairie and the adjacent restoration project Jim had worked on several years before.

When the steel plows went into that virgin prairie, chopping up the soil, they also cut down roots and rhizomes older than our old growth forests.

Bill and Fran proved a friendly couple with deep prairie roots. His family still owns the Smiley-Woodfin Meadow of more than two thousand acres, the largest remnant of unplowed tallgrass prairie in Texas. His father and uncle are descended from the Smiley family, who settled on a high prairie ridge west of Paris, the Lamar County seat of government, in the early part of the nineteenth century. But the place they thought I would want to see was a different one.

They had recently purchased a 110-acre horse farm near the small town of Melissa, in rural Collin County, and had been surprised to find within its borders a small cemetery established around the time of the Mexican War. "At first we were a bit unsure about having a cemetery on our property," Bill explained, adding, "but we were soon excited about it when we realized there were almost two acres of unplowed prairie there." It did not take me long to agree to pay them a visit.

The selected day was Father's Day, and a pleasant June breeze was blowing as I turned off the busy highway onto a small farm-to-market road that was once far out in the countryside near McKinney. The narrow and dangerously winding road snaked up one hill and down another, a relic from the era when motor cars traveled more slowly and roads were not imposed on the landscape but shaped by it. I passed several tall real estate signs posted beside weedy lands to catch the eyes of developers. Already roads and houses were being built nearby as urban sprawl stretched north from Dallas along Interstate 75 from Plano to Allen to McKinney. Soon it would reach the small town of Melissa. After passing a small church, I followed Fran's directions and turned onto an even smaller county road that had recently been paved with asphalt. A sign advertised 350 acres of prime development land for sale. Others signs were for smaller tracts, but all were destined to become row after row of houses as farmers scramble to get out from under the rising taxes that result from the high land values.

Coming to a T-junction, I turned right onto a white gravel road that inspired clouds of dust as I passed. I thought of Shel Silverstein's poem "Where the Sidewalk Ends." In a moment, with a mere turn of the steering wheel, I had reached a point to which the growing Metroplex had not yet extended, the place where the pavement ends. I took a deep breath. There were no telephone poles. I took another deep breath as I looked out at the broken outcroppings of white limestone covered in prairie flowers. Giant trees towered over the road on both sides, their greenery just waiting for the "for sale" signs.

At a silver gate, I again turned and was greeted by Bill, who came walking over a hill in work clothes. The June sunshine was powerful, but the breeze made walking pleasant. We soon caught up with Fran, and off we went to explore the property.

Honey locusts had taken over the pastures, they explained, and needed to be cleared. But fortunately, instead of raping the earth with a bulldozer to rid themselves of this thorny tree, an all-too-common practice that usually removes several inches of valuable topsoil, they had carefully cleared and then burned the locusts, which often invade overgrazed or abandoned fields. In so doing they had restored the open look of the prairie hills that rise from the creeks and streams, which bisect the landscape like fingers on an open hand.

In the floodplain along a nearby creek massive chinquapin oaks towered overhead, their leathery leaves shaped like ovals with tiny pinlike teeth along the outer edges. This tree, and its companion Shumard red oak, dominated the woodlands, as they often do in similar environs. Along the edges of the hillsides, water coursing through the deep creek has cut wide gashes into the earth, exposing the white rock that lies just under the surface. Although the barren limestone is blindingly hot in the summer sun, it is far from inhospitable. Dozens of prairie plants—some of them restricted to these areas—grow right out of the rocks. Some have found seams of moisture upon which they depend, their roots spreading through microscopic cracks like grass in a broken sidewalk.

In spring and summer the explosion of colorful wildflowers on these rocks is impressive, with pale coneflower, Barbara's buttons, blue wild indigo, and many others decorating what otherwise seems a desolate wasteland. Because they grow in areas too rocky and steep to plow, many of these plants survived the onslaught on the prairies, and their existence today is a fragmentary relict of Prairie Time. They create such a unique sight that some botanists think these rocky hillsides form a distinctive plant community in the Blackland Prairie—one dominated by wildflowers and not grasses.

Bill saved Stiff Cemetery for last. No roads lead to the graveyard. It is just an isolated island of prairie grass, a handful of trees and carved stones bounded by a chain-link fence. With the scent of hot cedars blowing in the wind and the lazy trills of cicadas singing in the bright sunshine, we opened the gate into this lost world. Although an employee of the cemetery association had just mown the grass, it was clear at once how remarkably well preserved the prairie was. Little bluestem was the dominant grass, extending across the hilltop like green carpet. Hundreds of coneflowers were visible—their roseate leaves evident in the cut grass—along with many more prairie plants, including a fascinating giant foxglove just outside the fence. Fran admitted that this was her favorite. The pale lavender crosses of prairie bluets waved on tall stalks, and bright yellow tickseed added June color to the landscape just as it did in 1847 when Jesse Stiff buried James, his fallen son.

Like so many other recent Texians, Jesse Stiff was a Virginian. His story is compelling because in it lies a behavioral blueprint, a history of Blackland Prairie settlement in microcosm. The story began in the tobacco fields of Virginia and worked its way westward through Tennessee to the cotton fields of Texas. It was driven by Eli Whitney's cotton gin, a simple device that brought such amazingly profound changes as to revolutionize the South.

The transformation of the Blackland Prairie of Texas began in Jamestown in the early seventeenth century with the cultivation of a plant sometimes referred to as that noxious weed (grown for money) and a grass named corn (grown for food). To grow tobacco required land—land devoid of trees and indigenous people. To grow corn required the same commitment—to annihilate the natives and the native vegetation and in their place to plant houses, fields, churches, and roads. This was the pattern that would later be transplanted to Texas by these God-fearing folk as they spread across the South.

The first cash crop had been tobacco, but later cotton found its way into the southern soil, at first mainly on the islands off the coast of the Carolinas, where a variety was grown that allowed the cotton seeds to be separated easily from the fabric of their lives. This variety did not thrive on the mainland, and because the seeds were tough to pick out of other varieties and required a great deal of energy, the fluffy white stuff remained local until a Connecticut Yankee named Eli Whitney moved down south to tutor the children of a plantation owner. His 1793 invention mechanized the separation process and breathed new life into cotton, compelling generations of young men and their families to move west.

Jesse Stiff was born in 1797 in Bedford County, Virginia, of English stock. He apparently came to Mexican-controlled Texas sometime before 1835, in search of opportunity. He married a girl of fifteen named Mary Feazle, and together they had at least two children, a son named James and a daughter named Rachel. Once freed of their Mexican overlords, who had outlawed slavery in 1830 and had demanded that settlers become Roman Catholic, the Texians celebrated their defeat of Santa Anna in 1836 with generous land grants to the heads of all families living the new Republic of Texas. Stiff was awarded a league of land that he claimed in 1838. His grant consisted of 4,605 acres northeast of McKinney on a rocky prairie, where he built a log cabin (which no longer stands) and began raising his family.

The United States annexation of Texas in December of 1845 provoked war with Mexico, causing Texas governor James Pinckney Henderson to leave office and mobilize regiments of fighting men whom he led into battle. Additional "ranging units," first created in the early days of the upstart republic by then president Sam Houston to maintain law and order, were pressed into service as scouts and light cavalry in the war against Santa Anna. Shortly after war was declared by the United States in May, 1846, the Texas Rangers included many volunteers who were eager to invade Mexico.

On the fourth of July in 1846, with war fever running as high as the temperature, Jesse and his son James enlisted in a company of rangers who planned to ride south and cross the Rio Grande. It would prove a grave decision, for the son would not live to see the end of the war. He was killed in 1847; historical accounts do not record the circumstances.

Perhaps as the father walked across the top of the prairie knoll he had owned for slightly more than a decade, something within him stirred. Perhaps he thought a prairie hillside awash in flowers—the deep cobalt bonnets of the blue wild indigo and the pale pink hats of the coneflowers—would provide a pretty setting in which to bury his son. Perhaps he wanted to look out across the meadow grasses from his front door and remember James. He dug the grave in the rocky soil not far from the cabin. Later as more people moved into the region, Jesse donated two acres for the cemetery that still bears his name and contains the graves of his family.

We were thankful for the breeze that warm Father's Day as we walked from the cemetery to the picnic tables under several old hackberry trees. Eating watermelon and marveling at the beauty of the place, we looked east across the hilltop while Bill and Fran explained how they hoped to use seeds harvested from the prairie grasses to restore their pasture to a prairie. Although no one has been buried in Stiff Cemetery since 1935, a small association still maintains it, keeping the grass mown and trimming the trees. Because the Woodfins own the land around the cemetery, they have been made association members. They hope to use their influence to suggest mowing the grass in July or August, after most of the flowers have seeded. Then they hope to rake the hay and scatter it across the hillsides, restoring the world that greeted Jesse Stiff when he surveyed this land and then surrounded it with fences to claim it.

A GIRL NAMED DAPHNE

The hand that built the firmament hath heaved
And smoothed these verdant swells, and sown their slopes
With herbage, planted them with island groves,
And hedged them round with forests.

> William Cullen Bryant, "The Prairies," 1832–33

Some of the . . . upland prairies . . . become lumpy (like
many of the Arkansas Prairies) where the interstices or flats
between the lumps are of a wet sandy cold soil. . . . These
flat lumpy prairies are quite similar in soil to the post oak
flats.

> Josiah Gregg, *Diary and Letters of Josiah Gregg*, 1841

WE stood on a road with no shoulders, staring at a green sign
that bore her name in white letters. Who was she? Every trace
of the community once called Daphne Prairie seemed to have
been packed up and moved away, like a movie set—a ghost town
forged in the pastoral countryside by a producer who wanted to
name the film after his daughter, perhaps?

*Prairies were viewed as fruitful only when they were eliminated and turned
into something useful.*

The silence was no less inspiring than the evening sky being rolled out for another sunset performance on this, the summer solstice, the longest day of the year. The tall grass—introduced, mostly—grew right up to the pavement, and we had to jump into that grass like rabbits to escape a speeding UPS truck that shattered the quiet. Kristin and I were learning how our companion, Jean Anne, had come to call the small county of Franklin home after living in Dallas. This had been her first prairie experience and she was impressed.

Our coterie included tour guide Bill Hicks, a Mount Vernon lawyer and one of the family stewards of this relic of antiquity; Bill takes pride in showing the towering mima mounds to visitors. Also along were Jean Anne's thirteen-year-old niece and Bill's long lost third cousin, Carla. We had taken a shortcut back to the road, and Bill and the others had volunteered to hike the remaining distance to the cars and pick us up.

On its eastern edge, the Blackland Prairies does not end abruptly; it fizzles out in an effervescent release of pressure that results in small bubbles of grass completely enclosed by woods. This is a land where tales of Cherokee Indians moving west ahead of the settlement frontier still excite romantic passions. It is a sandy land that seems as if it should not have had prairies, though somehow they remained long enough to be encountered by those who would give them Christian names and baptize them into the service of God and country. Black-and-white dairy cows graze in green pastures carved from dark forests, while Purple Martins buzz and chirp in the skies. Both the birds and the beasts reside in houses constructed for them by people who welcome their domestic tendencies. The birds are only half-domesticated—residing in white metal houses lofted into the air on long poles safely out of reach; the martins' pragmatism has put them on a footing almost equal to that of the barnyard animals.

As we approached Daphne from the south, cresting the top of a hill that seemed much higher once we were astride it, the view across the prairie called to mind pioneer accounts of pastures full of wild animals, like scenes out of Africa. "This is the start of the Daphne Prairie," Bill explained, one hand on the steering wheel and the other pointing out into the distance below us. From our vantage point the landscape looked diminutive—trees became small enough to grasp between two fingers. It was an inviting world, though the distances were deceiving, as we discovered when we got out of the car and begin walking.

Bill explained that the Daphne Prairie was once four miles long and two miles wide. It is mostly flat, surrounded by trees, and punctuated with the largest mima mounds known in Texas. As we emerged from the woods where we parked the vehicles, I was again reminded of early settlers who recorded their first impressions of prairies in language that harks back to the sea. These were unfamiliar places, and the tall grass made it hard to see the prairie for what it was. Giant coneflower—a tall brown-eyed Susan—is still the botanical king; its brown and yellow flowers perched on six-foot stalks.

We had taken a few steps into the grassy opening when something both bizarre and overwhelmingly magical happened, a kind of dream land prairie hallucination brought on by reading too many historical accounts of Prairie Time. The moment lasted perhaps ten seconds, but it left an indelible impression and a ray of hope.

The huge, dark, stunned bird jumped from the maze of tangled dewberries that choked out the small mima mound, stomping a few times to get its balance and to survey the threat that we presented. Then in a suddenness of flapping feathers and fleeing flight, the Wild Turkey mother launched into the air, reaching a height of ten feet or so before arcing back down to earth in the safety of a nearby wood. We gasped, we hooted, we hollered, and we exchanged excited and celebratory conversation.

It did not matter that this bird was likely the progeny of released birds, brought in from other states in cardboard boxes and set free. It did not matter that her parents or grandparents were immigrants in this land like our own—this bird represented a lost element that had returned to the prairies, a sort of prodigal. I thought of Thomas Howell's letter to his brother in June of 1852 from a small prairie opening not far from here as the crow flies, explaining how they had sent a Wild Turkey scurrying off a nest. For me the moment was pristine, a pinnacle of exaltation on the prairie, when I got more than a vicarious glimpse of the life that thrived in Prairie Time.

Wild Turkeys are still common in other parts of Texas, but the eastern population, which is a different subspecies from those in South and Central Texas and north to the Panhandle, was almost wiped out in an era of unrelenting hunting.

Buoyed by the sight of the turkey, we continued to tromp into the open meadow like sea-going travelers in a boat. The first part of our journey was through a large unplowed prairie remnant that is grazed by cattle. Our goal was an eighty-acre hay meadow that has not been trampled by grazing ungulates since buffalo roamed; it was fenced off. The Hicks brothers, John, Bill, and Sidney, and several cousins still own about three thousand acres of the original ten thousand acres first acquired by the Hughes and the Hicks families, who came to Texas during the brief interlude when it was a republic.

We pointed toward the strident calls of at least three separate bobwhites—announcing them to one another the way a child calls attention to every speeding police car rushing past with sirens blaring. The calls were a hopeful sign, a bit of exciting evidence that all the wildness in this world had not been stripped away. Meadowlarks exalted in the sunshine and Dickcissels chimed their incessant *djick, djick, djick . . . djick, djick djickcissel.*

We flushed dozens of these sparrows from the long grass where they hide their cup-shaped nests. Unlike the introduced House Sparrow (often called the English sparrow), these birds are native to the New World. The Dickcisssel sports a lemon yellow breast, rusty brown back and wings, and a gray and yellow striped face. The male wears a black triangular bib that is displayed prominently, particularly when the bird sings from a fence post or bush with his head thrown back and his chest thrust out like that of an athlete. In October these birds abandon the grassy prairies and old pastures with rank vegetation where they breed, enduring long flights to greener pastures in Mexico and South America, where they spend the winter. Their return in the middle of April is marked by the sudden appearance of thousands of birds trying to outperform one another vocally, signaling the start of another season of breeding in the prairies. The result is a chaotic wall of sound; a glorious expression of the abundance of bird life that once graced the prairies.

Dickcissels are among the few migratory prairie birds that still occur in such abundance on the Blackland Prairie—many others have been wiped out or greatly reduced in numbers. Perhaps this is because when the prairies were plowed these persistent creatures refused to give up, instead adapting to use agricultural fields of wheat and other grains to build their nests.

Today, though, they are threatened again—this time in South America, where farmers poison them by the thousands as punishment for eating seeds. There are graphic images of these birds, already unable to fly, twitching and turning on the ground in a slow death that takes several days to finalize.

As we walked in single file toward the long grass we kicked up a host of solitary Grasshopper Sparrows carefully spaced several dozen feet apart—a sign they were on territory and nesting. Each would fly a short distance barely above the grass before crash-landing into its secret world. They would relent and flush only when we nearly crushed them with our feet. Another sign that they were defending territory was their feeble attempts at song, a grasshopper-like trill that wafted across the breeze. The males sometimes deliver their warnings to other males from tall blades of grass, though often this message is conveyed from a secret hiding place.

They feast on a diet of grasshoppers, giving their name double meaning. Mousy birds, Grasshopper Sparrows often scamper about under the thatch—dead grass that remains from previous years—where their trails could be mistaken for those of rodents, a strategy that may make them all but invisible to a passing predator. Apparently they are more vulnerable to attack in winter; hence, like many grassland birds, these tiny creatures are adorned with buffy yellowish feathers, prairie camouflage that mimics the shades of winter's dead blades.

A few of these furtive birds remain almost unnoticed throughout the Blacklands all winter, lurking in pastures and old fields, but most disappear sometime in the autumn, after they have nested. In spring they return in late March or early April and males urgently commence the musical routines that advertise their presence to admiring females and competing males. Nesting begins soon afterward, with the females doing the domestic chores of nest building. She produces a domed structure with an opening on the side, resembling a Dutch oven woven of grass. Over a period of as many days she lays four or five eggs in this cryptic nest that will serve as home until the young fledge about a month later. Once they learn to fly she will nourish them for a few more days before they join a crowd of fellow fledglings in a flock called a crèche. In a few weeks they too will be able fly south, perhaps to Mexico or Central America, where they will seek grassy fields similar to those where they were hatched.

As we approached the tall grass, the mima mounds loomed like icebergs frozen in a sea of grass. We crossed the barbed-wire fence and hiked to the top of one. Almost as tall as a person, and larger than I remembered them from a visit a year earlier, they are arresting reminders of how much on Planet Earth we do not understand.

We studied the various grasses and wildflowers—little bluestem, azure sage, and a tiny pink flower with blossoms a millimeter or two in size called that could easily be overlooked: pink milkwort. We examined several white wild indigo plants that were already setting seeds in large black bean pods. The golden seeds, smaller in diameter than a BB, appeared ripe upon closer inspection of the pod's contents. A sudden burst of wings from underneath my feet revealed the cleverly woven nest of an Eastern Meadowlark. All of us took turns kneeling down to peer inside the tiny circular opening at the five white eggs placed inside; this was the first such nest I had ever seen.

Thirst made the trip back to the car seem a long one—and gave me a sense of the considerable size of this prairie opening. Although the line of green post oak trees where we had parked appeared to be no more than a couple of hundred yards away, it was in reality well over a mile distant. For the first time, I realized how big these island prairies had been and felt a twinge of the loneliness so often mentioned by pioneer travelers. In the absence of other landmarks, we used a distant dead tree as a navigational tool.

It occurred to me how comforting and reassuring even small objects, such as fences and fence posts, can become in the landscape. These grids imposed on the prairie help us relate to the world around us and serve perhaps as more than boundaries to mark property. Perhaps they are our way of coping with a world that is too big to understand. Perhaps they are our way of making the world smaller so that we can more easily find our place in it.

Perhaps, then, there was something unique about our pioneer ancestors who refused to chop down every tree, who refused to plow under every blade of grass. What impulses motivated some people to preserve the world around them in an era when doing so was terribly out of fashion? What traits did they possess that caused them to see the world as something that could be used without being completely destroyed? Such thorny questions puzzle me more and more as I grow older. Might searching for the answers to these questions allow me to uncover something about what still motivates people to conserve and to preserve? Perhaps in looking backward at those stalwart and courageous citizens I will find a way to convince people that our natural heritage is a precious part of who we are and an important legacy we leave to our children.

Later that evening I asked Bill to show me family photographs of his ancestors in the prairie. I hoped that answers to some of my questions could be gleaned from their faces and expressions. As I studied the black-and-white images of people and scenes faded to warm yellow like winter grasses, I realized that perhaps it would be easier to pinpoint Daphne's identity than to understand why some people in any era act to conserve rather than consume.

MANIFEST DESTINY

Our national birth was the beginning of a new history, the formation and progress of an untried political system, which separates us from the past and connects us with the future only; and so far as regards the entire development of the natural rights of man, in moral, political, and national life, we may confidently assume that our country is destined to be the great nation of futurity. Yes, we are the nation of progress, of individual freedom, of universal enfranchisement. Equality of rights is the cynosure of our union of States, the grand exemplar of the correlative equality of individuals.

John L. O'Sullivan on Manifest Destiny, 1839

AFTER spending time with her, I knew I wanted to see Daphne again, this time as the sun rose behind me. I wanted to see the sunlight cascade obliquely through her long hair, illuminating her form, highlighting her curves. I wanted to see her sleeping and I wanted to see her still partially clothed in dark-

The Blacklands originated in the sea, and like waves on an ancient sea, the surface of the black clay soil before it was plowed was rippled with formations known as gilgai.

ness as the budding new day gently awoke her from those slumbers. I had seen her at noon, when the harsh light of midday bore down upon her. I had seen her in the evening as she prepared for bed. But I had not seen her sleeping.

I wanted to see her pregnant with sunrise's expectation, with wonder, with delight—as she had been seen by the Caddo and Cherokee Indians who once celebrated the sunrise across her visage. I wanted to see the sun rise above her long grass as did Anthony Glass, the trader who in 1808 described the mima mounds and prairie-chickens, or as did those who followed; the first people with Christian names who brought their children to her to raise and brought their cattle to her to nourish and fatten.

Summer's long days and short nights cause daylight to come early. The first effects of sunrise—imagined traces, really—come when it still seems like the middle of the night. To be a witness to this daily miracle requires an even earlier rise from bed while the rest of the world sleeps. From sunrise to sunset days were once marked by the movement of the sun across the heavens—before ticking clocks dimmed its importance. This regular rising and falling defined the day, providing a sky full of symbolic meanings for life itself. Even now, sunrise is a time of new beginnings. The sky is alive with promise that electrifies the atmosphere. By contrast, sunset is a time of reflection, of saddened endings, and of thoughtful remorse. The prairies have witnessed them all, playing host to the proud dreams of people coming to take advantage of the grassland bounty.

To see Daphne awaken, I arose into a world still clasped firmly by the clutches of darkness. Soon the headlights of Mike Millican's car slowed and pulled into my driveway. Groggy, I climbed into the passenger seat, and we were on our way east to meet the coming day.

Mike is a Dallas attorney with whom I have several common interests, including birds and history. Racing down the interstate, alive even at that hour with glowing headlights rushing toward us in the darkness like lava flowing down a volcano, we passed through the sleeping towns of Cumby and Sulphur Springs. We took turns telling stories and discussing historical themes to pass the hour-long trip. As we came over a hill the city of Mount Vernon was shrouded in pale mist rising from the moist earth. The people of this small town were still sleeping as we exited the interstate. Continuing along a residential street, we passed through a pastoral neighborhood of homes built at least a century ago, and we approached the city square and the Franklin County Courthouse. On the lawn of that gray stone structure the pale statues of a naked Red Man and a Confederate Soldier, dressed neatly in uniform, shake hands—an unusual tribute to the defeated memories of men who died fighting for their own divergent lost causes, defending these fertile hills.

Once outside the small hamlet we turned again, heading east onto a narrow oil-topped road that marked the path of an ancient Cherokee road. After a few miles of winding through the picturesque countryside, we turned north on the paved road that leads toward the Daphne Prairie. Asphalt covers this little-known path along the Trail of Tears, which was used by the fleeing Cherokee Indians when Andrew Jackson expelled them from the United States in 1830. The Cherokee used it again when the Republic of Texas, under the leadership of Mirabeau B. Lamar, decreed that they would be forced north of the Red River and out of Texas.

The sky grew lighter by degrees as we reached the Daphne Prairie and began walking. Fragrant mists of dew lingered in the air and rose from the wet grass like a white veil slowly being lifted. Bird songs were playing in the background while the earth slowly turned its face toward the sun. Suddenly the darkness was gone. A golden ball appeared above the distant horizon, and the strident call of a surviving bobwhite exploded from somewhere in the grassy depths. Our legs were soaked to the knees as we traipsed through the large grayish green leaves of giant cone-flower, its yellow petals suspended above stalks that towered to six feet tall.

With the sun rising behind me, I wondered what it would be like to pretend that I was one of the first Anglo-Americans to walk across this opening in the forest. How would it feel to be a settler in the prairie, to stumble out of a dark forest into a grassy ocean for the first time? Noah Webster's 1828 masterpiece, *American Dictionary of the English Language,* did not even contain the word *prairie* because it is a foreign word borrowed from the French. I tried to imagine encountering these tall grasslands that stretch across the United States and struggling to force the tools of language to conform to what I was seeing. After traveling through dark forests and occasional clearings made by others with considerable expenditure of blood, sweat, and tears, these grassy openings carpeted with a riot of color and a rich profusion of tall grass would be a welcome sight. They would allow the good life without the effort of cutting down trees to plant crops.

Gazing across the grassy distance into the offing where the grass and sky became one unending entity that masked out the ribbon of trees marking the prairie boundary, it was easy to see how people could get lost in the liquidlike vastness that greeted travelers in Prairie Time. Even now, a visitor needs something like a distant tree as a beacon to keep from getting lost.

"This is a place where the signs are not written down but must be learned and studied," Mike suggested.

The sun was rising higher, the mist was beginning to fade away, and the sky was becoming bluer. The day was beginning to break wide open, spilling sunshine across the land like melted butter. We decided to sit for a spell. We needed a place to ponder these wide open spaces that seemed strangely out of place so far east in Texas. We paused in the prairie and watched the sun blaze a path across the heavens as the earth turned on its axis. We climbed to the top of a mima mound and listened to the incessant songs of the Grasshopper Sparrows and Dickcissels. An Upland Sandpiper whistled overhead, already flying south for the winter in the early July sky. Barn Swallows and Eastern Kingbirds darted past. A lone Scissor-tailed Flycatcher skirted by, long tail feathers in tow.

Mike noticed a male Eastern Meadowlark showing off on a nearby bush, advertising his presence not with song but with sudden jerks of his tail. We witnessed the bold defiance of several Grasshopper Sparrows defending their hard-won territories. I watched as one of these tiny tan-colored birds flew toward the sun, revealing a glint of gold as its wings caught the sunlight.

The baleful moans of cattle grazing on the unplowed splendor kept us company. A large healthy heifer the color of fall leaves slowly approached. Breathing heavily, sniffing the air, and dripping saliva, she continued to make her way toward us, curious about the strange interlopers sitting in her pasture. She came within five feet of us, and stood there with a quizzical look on her face for a few minutes before ambling off to chew her cud. There were no other signs or sounds of humans to remind us of this century. The engine of a distant airplane broke the spell briefly but then faded away, leaving us to relish our sense of being in another time. It was a time to think about beginnings, and perhaps about endings as well.

"Why were Americans drawn to this lonely, dangerous, and profoundly isolated wilderness even before it was a part of the United States?" I pondered aloud.

The standard answers to this question sometimes center around the concept of Manifest Destiny—that uniquely American concept coined in 1845 by editor John L. O' Sullivan. The process, however, was already well under way decades before the concept became the official justification for colonizing Texas and other western destinations all the way to the Pacific Ocean. By 1815, as the last salvos of the War of 1812 were being fired, the first Anglo-American settlers arrived in Texas by navigating the shallow, muddy waters of the Red River. These squatters must have been drawn to the small prairie openings on the southern bluffs of the river—in modern Red River County. By 1818 others had penetrated the forests toward prairie openings such as the Daphne Prairie—attracted, no doubt, to the free grass and the close proximity of tall timber.

Soon other restless folks were streaming in, bringing cattle and other livestock to graze on the grass—allowing them to roam freely on the open range. According to geographer Terry Jordan, in his *Trails to Texas*, this practice continued locally in Northeast Texas until well into the twentieth century, long after the introduction of barbed wire made the free range a thing of the past almost everywhere else.

As Texas began to fill up with people, there was one obstacle that had to be surmounted. Although the local Cherokees who had been pushed from their homelands in the southern United States had intermarried with the new Americans, adopting many of the settlers' ways, they were no longer welcome among the people of the young republic, who had just won their own freedom from Mexico. On April 10, 1841, the grasslands near the

Daphne Prairie just east of Mount Vernon became the scene of the last Indian massacre in eastern Texas. In one highly organized undertaking, Texans from as far away as Dallas banded together and chased these Native Americans from the area.

Thus the stage was set for a changing of the guard. As the newcomers took over, a host of new methods for obtaining food and shelter were employed on the prairies. Convinced of the superiority of their domestic cattle and chickens, these pioneers allowed ancient methods and the means of utilizing the bounty of the prairie to sink below the horizon. Although their extermination of many meat-giving creatures such as buffalo and turkey and prairie-chickens hastened this transformation from one culture to the next, the key element that symbolized this extinction of knowledge was the abandonment of methods of harvesting and preparing prairie plants for food and medicinal uses. As this information about how to survive slipped into obscurity, generations' worth of secrets teased from the earth through trial and error were lost.

Using our binoculars to bring them closer, Mike and I marveled at the massive mima mounds on the ungrazed prairie that has been saved by the Hicks family as a hay meadow. With binoculars compressing the distance between us and the mounds, they looked like violent waves on a storm-tossed sea. I could see the crests of the waves and half expected to see a tiny boat being tossed about, its lone occupant attempting to keep the vessel afloat in the storm. As we made our way toward the mounds, crossing through the fence that marks the grazed portions of the prairie from those that are never grazed, I could see that the mounds are in reality enormous piles of dirt and not waves. But what an impression they make; it is hard not to look at them and marvel.

Yet there are few people today who know or care about the presence of mima mounds. Still fewer are concerned with what Indians might have thought about them or how they could have used them. An exception is Linda Storm, a Washington native who became fascinated with similar mounds on Puget Sound and decided to take a year off from her job as a wetlands specialist to explore ways in which the Native Americans might have used these raised mounds in their daily lives.

A doctoral student at the University of Washington, she purchased a 1980s model Volkswagen van and loaded it with books and plant presses and enough basic necessities to be self-sufficient. Then, armed with a road atlas and some contacts around the country, she mapped out a strategy for crossing the United States on her quest to explore the prairies. This impulse is not entirely dissimilar to that of the hardy pioneers who loaded everything they could carry into a wagon and headed west onto the prairies. I offered to accompany Linda to other prairies with similar mima mounds one Sunday afternoon during her late May jaunt through Texas. Studying the mounds on the Daphne Prairie was a priority for her, because they are thought to be some of the largest in Texas, but also she was eager to see others, so I took her to the prairie at Gambill Goose Refuge west of Paris.

Besides offering well-drained sites on which to situate shelters or other forms of housing, she speculated, these mounds may have been used as sites for fire middens—pits dug into the earth and used for steam-roasting the bulbs of prairie plants. The process as she described it was remarkably simple. First a pit was dug into the soil and a large pile of wood was ignited. As the fire burned down to coals, rocks were placed on them. The roots of edible plants were then carefully wrapped in large fleshy leaves and placed atop the rocks before being covered with a deep layer of soil to keep heat and steam from escaping. After baking in this manner for two or three days, she explained, the nondigestible carbohydrate inulin (not to be confused with insulin) contained in the roots and bulbs was converted to fructose, which could be eaten.

As part of her research she was also gathering information about the edible plants that would have been available to local Indians. "Is there any camas here?" she asked as we roared off in her home away from home, *sans* air conditioning.

"Yes, we have a beautiful one called *Camassia scilloides*," I offered.

"Oh yes," she agreed, "that is a nice one. Do you think we can find some for me to collect?"

Sporting delicate blue flowers shaped like small stars that are arranged on the sides of stalks about eighteen inches tall, these plants are often an indicator of lands that have never been plowed. Her small trowel was no match for the tough clay sod as she rammed it into the earth around the waxy stem of the wild camas we found growing alongside a road surrounded with prairie grasses. After a disproportionate amount of effort for such a small reward, she finally retrieved the golf ball–sized bulb buried under eight inches of soil.

Native Americans were careful not to overharvest these bulbs so that they would not eliminate them from the landscape. "They were such valuable resources that people made sure they did not take the oldest bulbs—the largest ones, which produced more seeds each year—or the younger ones, which would be next year's harvest," Linda explained. Wisely, people took only medium-sized bulbs. They were also likely to have planted seeds, perhaps spreading the species and ensuring that the plants would be more widely available. Some ethnobotanists—people who study the relationships between indigenous people and the local flora—suggest that to a real extent, Native Americans were husbanding the resources within the landscapes they inhabited. It is an interesting idea, a possibility doubtless overlooked by the motorists who roared past while we examined the plants near the roadway. The notion of intentional plantings flies in the face of older interpretations stressing that these people were simply hapless hunter-gatherers who used what they could when it was available.

In this more recent view, fire was a particularly useful tool to the Indians. People deliberately ignited fires, ethnobotanists suggest, not only to attract game but to ensure that the prairie and its plants would remain, a position Linda wholeheartedly supports. Fire was not something to confine and to fear. It was something to unleash and to spread. As such it serves as a potent symbol of the divergence between the cultures that clashed on the Great Plains in the nineteenth century—one celebrating the freedom to roam and the other celebrating a more sedentary or confined lifestyle on farms or in towns.

Perhaps at an individual level the pioneer urge to move west has less to do with Manifest Destiny than with some very personal longings to be a part of, and to experience, the wilderness—to break out of a sedentary mold. Perhaps Manifest Destiny is only the sum total of millions of such quests to meet with such unbounded freedom. The American poet and nature writer Henry David Thoreau theorized that the people who are most wild are those who are most free.

If this is so, then it is among the reasons why birdwatching, hiking in places that are still wild, or canoeing through pristine lakes are so appealing to people who live in cities and work in boxed cubicles. Hitchhiking and living on the run to escape being caught or punished are darker manifestations of the urge for freedom from the civilized world. This same urge may be part of what motivates people like Linda to pack up and strike out on the road in search of glimpses of Prairie Time and of the people who experienced it.

THE BEE-LOUD GLADE

The Indians consider them [honeybees] the harbinger
of the white man, as the buffalo is of the red man; and say
that, in proportion as the bee advances, the Indian and the
buffalo retire.

Washington Irving, *A Tour of the Prairies,* 1832

I will arise and go now, and go to Innisfree,
And a small cabin build there, of clay and waddles made;
Nine bean-rows will I have there, a hive for the honey-bee,
And live alone there in the bee-loud glade.

William Butler Yeats, "The Lake Isle of Innisfree," 1893

THE sun was already well into the sky one balmy June morning when Bill Woodfin edged his blue pickup truck onto the side
of the narrow dirt road beside the pristine prairie that John Clayton once stewarded. Driving through the vast desert of cotton
and soybean fields that extended for miles around, it was easy to
see how this little patch offered a concentrated example of the

*Railroad corridors can be a source of rare prairie plants because they have
escaped the plow.*

diversity of life that was once taken for granted throughout the prairies. With a broad smile on his face, Bill eagerly changed out of his sneakers and laced brown leather hiking boots around his feet and ankles.

Thus appropriately shod, we set out to tread where traces of forgotten beauty would be loud with bird sound, loud with bee sound, loud with wild exploitations of color and displays of floral promiscuity where butterflies and birds and bees dance on tip-toes through forests of gayfeather swinging on prairie-scented breezes.

We crossed the ditch beside the dirt road, climbed into the prairie grass, and entered an ancient world. Multitudes of garden spiders had cast their homespun death traps, anchoring them to the hundreds of gayfeather spikes that arose from the moist earth. A nervous flittering of feeding butterflies fluttered past us, navigating through the lavender skyscrapers and desperately trying to avoid the spiderwebs thrown open for them. Several colorful wings dangling from the silky fibers bore witness to the risks involved in becoming so entangled.

Layered rays of sunshine filtered through a broken blanket of pale clouds. A breeze was blowing. Dew droplets were shining on lush green leaves, though the wind was busy smearing them into the atmosphere in humid oozes that reeked and lurched until they were felt beneath the skin like warm compresses pressed against sweaty flesh. The air was full of snowy seeds cast head-long into the breeze—each flying machine coded with life for next year's blooms.

The steady hum of thousands of native bees and wasps of many different species as well as various other flying creatures filled the air in all directions with the low drone of vibrating wings. The din began in the belly of the prairie and came surging forth like a rising chorus of massed choirs until, once aware of it, there was no getting the sound out of our awareness. Drunk on the sweet nectar of the prairie, the insects were oblivious to our presence. It was surreal, the kind of moment that forces medical doctors to become passionate Romantics.

"I will arise now . . . ," Bill began a thoughtful and elegiac recitation of William Butler Yeats's "The Lake Isle of Innisfree," in which the author sings the praises of the bee-loud glade where he wishes to make his home. Nineteenth-century poets often celebrated honeybees as symbols of nature's beauty. Yet, because of their meteoric spread throughout the continent after being brought across the Atlantic Ocean by immigrants, honeybees became a symbol of the spread of Anglo culture west across North America.

In fact, as American pioneers moved west onto the prairies beyond the Mississippi River (into terrain that contemporary maps labeled the Great American Desert), they found that honeybees had beaten them there. As they raided bee trees dripping with honey, they could not help but conclude that they were settling a land of milk and honey. In 1832 Washington Irving visited the prairies in what is today Oklahoma, penning his adventures in *A Tour of the Prairies.* Two years later, he related that the Indians described the bees as the "harbinger of white man," while he concluded that they were "the heralds of civilization."

That same year editor-in-chief of the *New York Evening Post,* William Cullen Bryant, traveled to Illinois, where he viewed the prairie's "airy undulations" for the first time. He began his poem "The Prairies," which celebrated that encounter, with a loud and clear message refuting the notion that the prairies were deserts. With a touch of sarcasm and some measure of irony, he proclaimed: "These are the gardens of the Desert, these unshorn fields, boundless and beautiful." Bryant, too, noticed the honey-bees, and found in them a symbol for the Americans who would soon overspread the prairies. His conclusion contains a percep-tive prediction:

> . . . The bee,
> A more adventurous colonist than man,
> With whom he came across the eastern deep,
> Fills the savannas with his murmurings,
> And hides his sweets, as in the golden age,
> Within the hollow oak. I listen long
> To his domestic hum, and think I hear
> The sound of that advancing multitude
> Which soon shall fill these deserts.

The prophetic nature of Bryant's poem was apparent as we stood there, isolated like castaways on a small island in a vast desert of plowed fields. Despite the small size of this prairie, I have re-turned many times to walk upon the ancient soil and to feel the wind course through my hair and to hear the bees buzzing in my ears. It is not a place to imagine wide prairie vistas or sweeping landscapes. But I come here because it is a place where today is erased, and the past can be placed quite close up in my face as though I were viewing it through a macro lens. It is a lens I have wished for many times.

The following September I returned to the bee-loud glade with Austin ethnobotanists Scooter Cheatum and Lynn Mar-shall. Their goal was to photograph a rare Texas wildflower named stiff sunflower for inclusion in their monumental twelve-volume series *The Useful Wild Plants of Texas*. Scooter and Lynn are researching and documenting the usefulness of over four thousand plant species that occur in Texas—many of them prairie natives about which little has been published. It is a Herculean task that has already consumed nearly thirty years of their time.

When we arrived, we discovered how resilient prairie plants can be even after three cruel months of Texas summer sun baking the soil and opening deep cracks in the earth. A few bees still buzzed and a spate of butterflies still fluttered by. However, an entirely new suite of plants was blooming, including sizable drifts of the conspicuous stiff sunflower.

Known to science as *Helianthus pauciflorus* (meaning "few-flowered," a reference to the fact that not all of the plants bloom each year), it grows to a height of three or four feet or more and sports long, pointed leaves that droop lazily from a thin purple stem. The upper portion of the plant bends over ever so slightly under the weight of the yellow disc and ray sunflowers that hang shyly in all manner of awkwardness. Yet it is a sociable plant, on account of its creeping rhizomatic roots that allow it to form sizable colonies, though botanists have collected it from only a handful of sites in Texas. Undoubtedly it was once more common in the clay soils of the Blackland Prairie, before plowing nearly eliminated it. In fact, it is not absent from even a single square foot of this prairie remnant. Because it maintains a quiet dignity through the heat of summer, before calmly bursting into flower in September, it has become one of my favorite wildflowers. And because there is plenty of moisture in the soil here, it fails to live up to its name: almost every single plant is decorated with three or four bright yellow sunflowers.

According to Scooter the tiny sunflowers, like most species in this genus, are edible—though they are so small that separating the seeds from the hulls would be a chore to all except the birds that visit the dried seed heads in winter for a meal. We know little about how the Native Americans may have used this plant. The thick leathery leaves are rough, like sandpaper, and once the winter chill dries them they become extremely tough; perhaps the Indians had a use for them.

In late November I returned to see how the dried flowers had arranged themselves and to study and collect a few stiff sunflower seeds. The prairie was mostly silent—tucked in for the winter—and the bee-loud glade was but a memory. A lone gulf fritillary fluttered uneasily through the towering stalks of gayfeather and stiff sunflower.

The prairie seemed lonely. The sky was gray and summer's exuberance had been replaced with a somber beauty that grows on me the more I contemplate it. As I bumped into the tall stalks, the patient seeds of the gayfeather literally exploded into the air and fell into the thick grass. They will need more patience, I figured, if their plan is to lie dormant in the cool darkness until a fire rages over them, or a herd of buffalo passes this way and grazes the thick grass, finally letting sunlight reach the seeds and allowing them to sprout.

Patience is something I have learned from watching the prairie. The flowers must be appreciated when they are blooming, and the seeds must be harvested when they are ripe. The bee-loud glade will return when it is time. Yet even as the season was winding down for another year, the next one was in the planning stages.

Underneath the soil, the stringy white rhizomes of stiff sunflowers were spreading outward in search of new places to spring up next spring. Already the tender leaves of many prairie plants were just emerging from the still warm soil, including the floppy elephantine ears of *Rudbeckia maxima*. These seemingly tender leaves remain green all winter, shrugging off even the coldest freezing temperatures, as they harvest sunlight and ferret it into their roots as energy. As soon as the days begin to warm, this stored energy is used to send the tall stalks towering skyward and to produce new leaves that will further aid the plant in the culmination of its existence—flowering.

These are the natural rhythms of life that dictate how the prairie coexists with the life around it. And being a witness to— or perhaps even a part of—this majestic drama is the reason I return. I come for more than merely knowing the names of the plants or seeing them in their natural communities. I come to feel the natural world ebb and flow around me in a cosmic swirl that defies my understanding.

PRAIRIE HARVEST

The herbage of the Prairie being plentiful and nutritious, the farmer considers that no additional feeding is necessary. . . . By mowing the grasses when ripe, and stacking it near their homesteads on the Prairie, they would have a wholesome provender stored for the winter, without any expense except labour, and their cattle would keep in good condition throughout the winter season.

John Barrow, *Facts Relating to North-Eastern Texas,* 1849

The big doors of the country-barn stand open and ready,
The dried grass of the harvest time loads the slow-drawn
wagon,
The clear light plays on the brown gray and green
intermingled.

Walt Whitman, "Leaves of Grass," 1855

WATCHING prairie hay being cut is not exactly a spectator sport. It is certainly not the kind of activity that will fill a stadium. Perhaps, it occurs to me, watching the tall grass being

Looking at old photos raises the question of why some people in any era act to conserve rather than consume.

cut is not even normal. But when Mr. Garrett called me early one morning shortly after our nation had celebrated its birthday, I could hardly resist the invitation.

"The forecast is calling for three or four days of dry weather," the voice on the telephone explained. "We'll start cutting the 'med-ah' this afternoon, if you want come down and watch."

Prairie hay cutters are my heroes. They took up the slack when fire was eliminated from the prairies and kept the invading trees at bay. I doubt any have ever been thanked for the gift they have left us. Their deliberate and laborious routines, fleshed out of sweat and blood each year for generations, have ensured that we can walk in dream land. We have tall grass to watch waving in the wind because they valued an art form passed down from the earliest pioneers. Because of them, we can experience the rush of a prairie and sing along with the symphony— adding our voices to the diversity— of celebrants who have extolled the beauty of prairies over the eons. Without their loving care, these prairies would have vanished in one way or another as trees marched steadily like an invading army into the prairie. How could I turn down the opportunity to watch history being made?

The July sun was already blazing down on the freshly cut grass when I arrived. Howard was wearing his white straw hat and pulling a hay rake with a vintage 1954 red and gray Ford tractor. He rode over to greet me and killed the engine. I waved at his brother David, who was astride a green and yellow John Deere towing a giant yellow hay baler that looked more like some prehistoric dinosaur than like a piece of farm equipment.

"Make yourself at home," Howard offered. "We have a boy over there mowing who is a high school senior at Miller Grove," he added, pointing in the direction of a couple of oak mottes. "You may want to get some pictures of him cutting the meadow."

The annual routine of cutting the prairie had just begun. I do not know why, but first I wanted to see the green grass still waving freely in the breeze. I wanted to see the prairie once again before it became fodder for farm animals the following winter, when the freezing wind whipped across the prairie and the trees stood naked. In high summer, with sunscreen smeared over every exposed surface of my skin and forming big drops under the shelter of my baseball cap, it was more than a small challenge to comprehend the frigidness of winter. It was hard to imagine zipping up my heavy coat and stepping out into a blowing norther, hard to remember the wind biting into my face, causing tears to form in my eyes. But anticipating the changing seasons was critical to survival in the prairies. To beat the unforgiving elements meant winter's cold had to be anticipated in the heat of summer. There was no time to sit in the shade. July hay had to be baled when it was ready.

But today was a day for learning, for observing, for watching how prairies are preserved today without flames. Although the roar of the tractors pacing back and forth was ever present, I became lost in my own thoughts as I wandered through this green pasture of wire grass that blankets the sandy soil like a fine carpet. I admired the unusual white ball blossoms of rattlesnake master, its long leathery leaves resembling those of a yucca. I studied the Canada wild rye, its V-shaped seeds already golden brown and ready to be scattered. I wandered, without aim, without goals, without even being aware that I was indeed planting both feet on the ground. I was in dream land.

Finally, I headed back toward the action. I found a lone oak on the meadow and, positioning myself in the shade, made a seat out of the fresh prairie grass already cut and laid neatly on the ground. From my vantage point it appeared that the Garrett brothers were going round and round in circles. Howard, on the smaller gray tractor, was raking the cut hay into neat piles called windrows. David, on the larger green tractor, was scooping the piles of grass into the yellow baler—occasionally pausing to disgorge the large round bales that were belched out of the machine's big mouth. I imaged the play by play of the event: "Here comes David on the green tractor—oh, he is stopping to let out another bale. Wow, look at all that dust!"

It was a perfect day for cloud watching, an almost forgotten pastime that once kept children and adults alike entertained on hot summer days. Small white clouds, puffy like popcorn, passed lazily in the light blue sky as cicadas droned and moaned. One cloud resembled a baby bird still in the nest, unable yet to fly— until it morphed into a candidate for a Rorschach test. A dust devil played with the freshly cut hay, whipping grass and dust into its cyclonic grasp.

Now was the time of day when the birds take a well-deserved siesta. Even the buzzards were not very busy; they wheeled about, gently rocking back and forth, looking as if they hoped they would not spot something dead to eat. A Red-bellied Woodpecker made several trips back and forth overhead along some unseen highway mapped out only in its mind—white wing stripes flashing in the sun as the bird passed by in silent undulations.

I surveyed the way the land was shaped, slightly sculpted to funnel rainwater into the creeks from the sandy grass-covered hills. I looked for patterns in the shapes of the oak mottes that sequestered, that sheltered, that bent over and touched the earth like the twisted landscapes of Thomas Hart Benton. The earth itself, in that vivid landscape of colors—bright yellow, grass green—flowed seamlessly into an image that curved inward to wrap itself around me. The horizons became warped, the hillsides buckled, the trees gnarled. The sky and the clouds collapsed to become a part of the vortex. Suddenly I was sitting under a tree watching men with scythes cutting hay in another century. A scarab crawled in the sand. White flowers grew from the shade of a twisted tree. Men as much shaped by the landscape as they were shapers of the landscape moved in rhythmical, backbreaking movements.

I was awakened from my vision of the past by the sound of a tractor coming toward me—another green John Deere armed with a long cycle blade that sliced into the grass a few inches above the ground. As the high school kid bounced along on the prairie, the blade would occasionally knife into the ground, sending up sudden explosions of pale dust that looked like the powder smoke from colonial era muskets being shot. In the pastoral landscape, I could imagine armies firing the temperamental weapons, the smoke evident along a line as they fired in succession. I could hear the distant hum of the tractors going around in circles, droning off in the distance as they as drove away.

It has been suggested that art, like form, should follow function. If so, then prairie hay cutting is indeed an art form. Although the tools and the instruments have changed over time, the relationship with the elements, with nature, remains unchanged. Like potters who depend upon the shapes already in the clay to help them form their wares, or a sculptor who sees shapes hidden in stone and takes off just enough material to reveal the vision, prairie hay cutters use nature's bounty to find a fruitful harvest.

After a while I heard Howard's Ford tractor idling my way. "Would you like some water?" he offered in a weak voice. He was tired; the heat was clearly taking its toll. But he had something more important than water to offer me. Riding around all day on a tractor gives a man time to think—time to think about the past, about now, and about the future. Perhaps in the heat of the day when the sweat makes one thankful for a breeze, they all become one. His words were reflective. He was in charge of his memories of the meadow. Although they were his possessions, he wanted to share them with me. He wanted to pass them on, to make a small part of them mine.

"This used to be the only hay meadow of *any* kind around here," he began. "People used to work all day for six bales a day so they could feed their cattle. But there were no Bermuda grass pastures then. If we found a sprig of it we hoed it out," he added. His string of remembrances could hardly do justice to describing the thoughts that must have crossed his mind as flashes of a life lived on the prairie.

With a wave of his hand, he changed the subject. Pointing west toward the direction of the sun when it sets, he let me in on a secret. He was trying to form some mental picture of Prairie Time in his own mind, and then show it to me, using the imperfect medium of language. "The grass on this bald prairie used to stretch that way all the way for miles," he intimated, revealing perhaps more of what he really thinks about as he bounces along on the prairie all day.

I had to ask because I wanted to understand what he meant. "Why did they call it a 'bald' prairie?"

My question was genuine, because to me his prairie seemed to have a rich healthy head of long green hair.

His reply was clear, simple, and meaningful: "Well, I guess it was because it didn't have trees on it."

THE TALLGRASS
CAPITAL OF TEXAS

...The hills
Rock-ribbed and ancient as the sun,—the vales
Stretching in pensive quietness between;
The venerable woods—rivers that move
In majesty, and the complaining brooks
That made the meadows green; and, poured round all,
Old Ocean's gray and melancholy waste.

William Cullen Bryant, "Thanatopsis," 1814–21

A few miles to the eastward of Paris, the capital of Lamar county, the country is highly picturesque. The undulating prairies are of comparatively small extent, confined with belts of timber on innumerable streams; the land is high and dry, and the herbage composed of a variety of grasses of luxuriant growth.

John Barrow, *Facts Relating to North-Eastern Texas*, 1849

WHEN I was young I spent a lot of time with my grandma. She would sit in a chair while I played with my toys, listening to her stories. She was the mother of my father, and having been born in 1893—a mere three years after the official closing of the frontier—she had been raised in a world very different from mine. Wild Indians still excited her fears (a condition that grew worse as she aged), and in her stories the "Injuns," as she called them, still seemed as real as they had indeed been to her and the people who had instilled this fear in her.

Her stories were a living link to people who were born before the Civil War, and though I did not realize it at the time, they offered valuable insights into the peopling of the Blackland Prairie. One story she told often was that of her own grandmother, who fell ill on the already well-worn trail that connected Tennessee to the promise of Texas. About five years before the War Between the Sides, she and her family were going west, following their dreams into the sunset with their belongings crowded into a wagon (they were likely on foot). They reached the Red River, where they almost certainly crossed on a ferry and then struck out through the red clays hills girded with towering forests. They had just come out onto the prairies east of Paris—a prairie so beautiful it had been named Blossom for the array of flowers that blossomed there—when she departed this life, leaving a newborn child without breasts to suck.

The grassy landscape in which this unwritten drama unfolded was portrayed in the diaries of the famous frontier naturalist and explorer Josiah Gregg, who described the Blossom Prairie a few years earlier. "Blossom Prairie," he said, "is generally from 4 to 5 or 6 mi. wide from E. to W. The most of the north of this prairie is of the black soil covered with rosin weed—but a good deal of the South is of a cold gray unproductive soil—inclined to be wet and covered with *wire grass.*"

That motherless child's name was Brittania, and she was my grandmother's mother. What happened next is perhaps the reason she always insisted that "colored" people be treated with respect—a rare trait indeed on the Blackland Prairie in an era when lynchings were still meted out without the merest twinge of trepidation.

Somewhere along that road a slave woman with an infant of her own took my great grandmother and nourished her. At that crucial moment, which before formula and baby bottles could well have meant the difference between life and death for the child, color was not important—though, in fact, such arrangements were more frequent in those days. The notion of this woman of bondage cradling and giving life to an infant who would later give birth to my grandmother must have had an impact on Grandma. She often told how they continued their journey to the heart of the Blackland near the community of Clinton, in Hunt County, only after her grandmother had been hastily buried in the prairie near the small community of Blossom in Lamar County.

With more acres of unplowed tallgrass prairie soil than any other Texas county—though no highway signs advertise this distinction—Lamar County is the tallgrass prairie capital of Texas. This county on the northern terminus of the Texas Blackland Prairie, on the spine between the Red River and the North Sulphur, is home to a scattering of native hay meadows including the crown jewel, the grand champion of them all, the Smiley-Woodfin meadow.

One hot summer day, Bill Woodfin and I decided to pay these prairies a visit—to make our own tour of the prairies. Our first stop was the meadow that bears his family name, located a rifle shot from the little town of Brookston, a small gathering of homes nestled on a scenic rock-ribbed prairie ridge named for the narrow brooks that originate here. Flowing in opposite directions, these small intermittent creeks become the tributary streams for both the Red and the North Sulphur. The largest buildings in the town are two giant barns—warehouses, really—for the hay harvested every June and July from the Smiley-Woodfin Meadow.

"We used to load the hay onto the train right there," Bill explained, pointing to a long narrow grassy lot beside the railroad tracks, across the street from where the downtown business district had been planted. In its heyday this was a neat row of brick buildings. Today a mix of empty lots and a few small houses fill the void, the emptiness apparent to anyone who recalls the bustling enterprises and busy people working hard to make money from the black land. He looked out of the open window, reflecting as we motored away, the breeze rearranging the heat. "The hay was loaded onto trains and hauled all the way to Fort Bliss in El Paso," he told me as we turned a corner and headed north. "They used it to feed the horses in the cavalry."

We passed three or four houses and then turned again onto a gravel road and into a large barnyard with two massive silver barns, each about the size of a football field. The sweet smell of hay met us first—a rich organic aroma that is one part prairie meadow blowing in the breeze and two parts sugar with a pinch of basil thrown in for spice. We loaded several square bales from the barn into the back of his pickup and then for nostalgia's sake drove the loaded vehicle over the unattended scales, where customers purchasing hay get it weighed so that they can be charged by the pound.

"I worked in there during the summer of my fifteenth year," he said, pointing to a small white frame building next to the scales.

After a short drive north to the hinterland outside Brookston, we discovered the gate that Bill's cousin Mack had left
open for us. Mack lives nearby in Paris and manages the
meadow but was unable to join us on this visit. To drive through
the gate was to cross the threshold, crossing over into Prairie
Time, a grand escape from the world of diesel trucks and speeding cars flying by in linear oblivion to the scenery a short distance away over the next hill. We made our way to the top of the
highest hill and ate our picnic lunches, while I read passages
from Washington Irving's *A Tour of the Prairies*. Parallel waves of
eastern gamagrass twisted in the wind where they grew in the
narrow troughs that drained the unplowed, uneroded hillsides
rolling before us.

To stand in this prairie and behold the scenery unfolding before me was a moving experience—a true soul vacation. It was
as close to standing on a mountaintop and looking out over the
rarified air as one can get in the lowlands. Here, with an unbroken blue sky overhead, the land below was as a seamless as the
ocean, punctuated only by the incipient beginnings of Pine
Creek, which snaked northeastward and formed a green ribbon
of small trees that melted into the pale horizon. Somewhere in
the distance the creek issues its cargo into the Red River, mixing
the relatively plentiful prairie rainfall of these hills with scarce
and valuable water from thunderstorms on the high plains, water that could have fallen five hundred miles to the west.

Before yielding to that giant of a river, this relatively humble
tributary creek has some business of its own to take care of. Leaving the prairie behind it enters a world where dark forests rest in
a broad flat river bottom carved from sandy hills covered with
post oaks, blackjack oaks and shagbark hickories, sassafras trees
and flowering dogwoods. As it meanders closer to the Red River,

Pine Creek widens, gains momentum, and cuts through steep hillsides of black Woodbine Sand—an ancient geological formation that crumbles as it sheds its dark secrets—creating jagged bluffs that mark the nearly buried southernmost extension of Arkansas' Ouachita Mountains, and covered with giant chinquapin oaks, Carolina basswood, Carolina buckthorn, and a host of other trees. A rare shrub called mock orange lives nowhere else in Texas and clings tenuously to survival near where Thomas Howell heard the raucous screams of Carolina Parakeets in 1852.

Once thrust into the red-stained torrents and eddies of the Red River, water from Pine Creek becomes indistinguishable from runoff of any one of a thousand such feeder creeks in four states. As part of this larger river thick with suspended sediments, the prairie rainfall is hurled eastward, toward Shreveport and beyond. Later it will flow into the mighty Mississippi, where it is funneled through the levees that keep it out of New Orleans, and in one last thrust it enters the Gulf of Mexico, where its sediments are deposited in the delta. As this fresh muddy water is flushed hundreds of miles into a water world where Sooty Terns and Magnificent Frigatebirds dine on the organisms its nutrients support, the water from the prairies may be sucked into the Gulf Stream, where it will cross the Atlantic Ocean and warm the British Isles the following winter. Or perhaps it will evaporate into the atmosphere and be blown inland again across Texas by a hurricane. There it may fall on thirsty soils and be absorbed into underground aquifers, or it may fall in torrents so heavy that it will run off and continue its restless journey, again seeking the sea.

Like a fluid interstate highway system, the Mississippi River played an important role in linking the growing nation together and facilitating the fulfillment of so many dreams to conquer the continent. Until boats powered by steam-driven engines were developed, early travelers on the river and its tributaries were mostly dependent on the river to carry goods downstream to New Orleans. There they could be sold and loaded on sailing vessels for shipment to ports around the world.

The invention of steamboats helped open the vastness of the interior of the United States to two-way trade and was nothing short of a transportation revolution. Like platelets and blood cells the ensuing traffic coursed its way through the veins of the Mississippi and the rivers flowing into it—changing forever the prairies on the Great Plains. A logjam, however, blocked the Red River and prevented steamboats from roaring up its waters. Loose soil on the banks of the Red often gave way as floodwaters ate into them, undermining the roots of large trees and toppling them into the water before carrying them away, twisting and turning in the currents.

When the floating trees reached what is now Shreveport, Louisiana, they were halted by rush hour traffic. Too many logs trying to squeeze through the narrow river produced gridlock, creating a permanent delay in the form of a great raft that is reported to have stretched upriver for well over a hundred miles. As the downed trees became wedged into place, sediments were deposited onto them, forming soil that sprouted yet more trees.

A wandering of drifters and a scattering of squatters began seeping into Spanish Texas from Arkansas and settling along the Red River (at the risk of imprisonment) even before the Adams-Onis Treaty with Spain in 1819 set the boundary between the two nations as the Red River. For a time, both the United States and Spain claimed the territory. Following the treaty, though, many Americans continued to assert that the regions drained by the Red and the Sulphur rivers were actually obtained from France in 1803 as part of the Louisiana Purchase.

Shortly after Mexico ousted its Spanish rulers in 1821 the young government issued an invitation to Americans to settle Texas and convert the untamed wilderness into productive farms and cities. Vainly attempting to retain some control over the settlement process, Mexican authorities solicited the help of land agents called empresarios, who were to be responsible for luring families into the region. Some, like Stephen F. Austin, successfully installed a number of families. But most of two dozen or so empresarios failed to accomplish their goals before Mexico retracted the welcome mat to settlement in 1830.

After finishing my lunch, I climbed into the bed of Bill's pickup and stood atop the hay bales for a better view of the landscape that stretched forth like it did when Mexico hoped to bring loyal Catholics to these virgin soils. Here, perhaps more than any other place in Texas, it is possible to behold a panoramic vision of Prairie Time in a land that inspired some grand schemes to make fortunes. Surveying the rolling hillsides from my elevated vantage point, I begin to think of my own distant relative Benjamin Rush Milam and his good friend Arthur Goodall Wavell, who together hoped to subdue this wilderness. Grandma often spoke of Benjamin, though the family stories never mentioned his failed venture in northern Texas.

A Kentucky native born in 1788, Milam served in the War of 1812 before striking out to make his fortune. He floated south to New Orleans, planning to sell a raft load of grain. Unsatisfied with the prices he was offered, he joined several others and from there sailed to South America looking for more profitable offers. Apparently succeeding in taking leave of the cargo, he returned to Texas and by 1818 was on the Colorado River trading with the Comanche Indians. Becoming a Mexican citizen, he joined the Mexican Revolution and was made a colonel; for his services in that effort he was awarded eleven leagues of land, though he mistakenly placed his claim in Arkansas before the error was realized, forcing him to relocate a bit farther west.

In 1825 Milam talked his friend and business associate General Wavell into applying for a land grant between the Red River and the Sulphur River—a vast territory stretching from the prairie headwaters of the Sulphur to where it empties into the Red. A consummate opportunist and a chronic soldier of fortune, Wavell was born in Scotland in 1785 and later fought for a string of countries including England, Spain, Chile, and Mexico. In 1826 Mexico awarded Wavell his request, although some of the land he was planning to populate was actually in the United States. Later that year he attempted to visit his colony in the northern reaches of Mexico but was prevented by floodwaters on the Red. Another intended visit was forestalled in 1831 by a bout of rheumatism.

Milam agreed to become Wavell's agent, while Wavell planned to publicize the venture in England—though he was faced with the daunting task of recruiting Protestant citizens to move to an isolated corner of Catholic Mexico without ready access to the outside world. The task of luring settlers would prove even more difficult after 1830, when Mexico undermined the entire colonization process by banning the immigration of Americans into Mexico—a blow that must have been devastating to those empresarios who had incurred substantial debts in the schemes. That same year the government outlawed slavery. No doubt frustrated by these obstacles, in 1831 Milam purchased a steam ship named the *Alps* and, during a brief period when the river was running high, navigated it past the jam on water being diverted around the logs. Finally someone had found a way onto the waters of the upper Red River and into the heart of Wavell's colony.

In the face of these odds Milam continued working to bring families into the Red River region. He traveled to Monclova, the capital of Coahuila and Texas, to persuade Agustín Viesca, the governor of the region, to allow the settlers to obtain title to their land. Although Viesca agreed to do this, Milam was thrown in jail; he soon escaped and become embroiled in the Texian effort to overthrow the inglorious regime of Santa Anna. Milam did manage to bring 140 families to Wavell's colony, but his assassination in San Antonio in 1835 would prove fatal to the fledgling enterprise. Nevertheless, by showing that it was possible to bypass the clogged arterial valves of the Red River's heart, Milam set in motion a world of changes that would be the undoing of Prairie Time in the northern reaches of Texas.

In 1833, just two years after Milam navigated around the raft, the city of Clarksville was established and the region began to attract people. By 1840 so many people were pouring into the fertile prairie lands south of the Red River that Lamar County had to be carved out of Red River County.

After touring the Smiley-Woodfin Meadow and Tridens Prairie, Bill and I concluded our tour on a prairie with soil so sandy and so red that it takes a healthy measure of faith to believe it is actually part of the Blackland Prairie. As the crow flies the Gambill Goose Refuge is only three miles from the vast open highlands of the Smiley-Woodfin Meadow. However, Gambill is a prairie cloistered by oaks—southern red oak, post oak, water oak, and willow oak—because it is situated in the openings between the fingerlike creeks that drain into Sander's Creek. An extraordinarily beautiful prairie, Gambill provides a rare glimpse of the world that greeted early settlers.

Many years ago a small dam was built on Sander's Creek, and the water that backed up behind it is called Lake Gibbons. The surrounding refuge is named for the Canada Geese that remain all summer and are supplemented in fall and winter with wilder kin of several species that come honking from the north to graze in the small plowed field planted with grain for their benefit. Some of the people who come to fish the lake's waters do not think the signs that prohibit driving on the prairie apply to them. In places ruts gouged into the soil make the red earth appear wounded and bleeding. Near the boat ramp discarded chunks of concrete debris from a destroyed roadway are piled high on the prairie like a cairn, as if in a concrete monument to the buffalo bones that were once piled high.

Abuse and neglect notwithstanding, this burgeoning prairie contains a wonderful juxtaposition of plants from two different prairie communities. Eastern gamagrass and switchgrass grow side by side with Silveus's dropseed and Mead sedge—in some places sedge and dropseed outnumber the grasses, while in other portions the pattern is just the reverse. Apparently this prairie lies on what was once the rough boundary between the prairies that thrived on black soil and those that clung to the sandy red soil along the Red River.

Before we ended our tour, Bill and I watched crows passing over—their high-pitched nasal *cah-cah, cah-cah* repeated in doublets identified them as Fish Crows, a smaller cousin to the familiar and widespread American Crow. Once confined to the swampy coastal woods, Fish Crows have begun following the Mississippi River well inland, navigating their way along the major tributaries and even the smaller feeder streams onto the edge of the prairie itself, rather like the early pioneers. We counted seventeen birds in one flock and about eighteen in another. In the last decade these birds have been moving west along the Red River, following many of its tributary creeks north almost to their sources. As people have dammed the rivers, creating lakes, these opportunistic members of the corvid family have spread well inland to dine on fish, and they also take other small creatures.

We took time to smell the flowers and to study them. Scattered among the entries in this exhibition of nature's floral arrangements were the showy purple flowers of a mint called wild bergamot. In Texas it is called horsemint because its crushed leaves and flowers smell uncannily similar to the aroma of a horse. Botanists refer to it as *Monarda fistulosa*, and during the American Revolution, when the colonists' tea leaves of choice were not available, a home-brewed tea was made from the pungent leaves. We saw another plant once brewed the same way and today found only in prairies: New Jersey tea plants had already bloomed and were now setting small round black seeds where the little white blossoms had been.

It may seem unusual that colonists on the eastern seaboard used these two natives of the Blackland Prairie, but as ecologists point out, few plants occur only in the tallgrass prairie and nowhere else. Most also occur in forested openings in the east, and some, like these two, grow all the way to the Atlantic Ocean.

As we wandered, taking in the beauty and serenity of this dream land, Bill and I stopped to study a milkweed. A favorite of his and of the butterflies that flitted about, this plant is named for the milky substance that leaks from the plant when a leaf is picked. The seeds are contained in long hornlike pods that break open when they are dry, the prairie breezes then scattering the fluffy seeds to the four winds.

Even though it was late June, the floral fireworks were not yet over. One of the most common flowers on this prairie would soon be blooming; we recognized the plant called ashy-leaf sunflower by its gray-green leaves. By careful searching I managed to find a handful of these yellow gems blooming early—unlike most sunflowers, the sunny faces were nodding away from the sun. We also found a purple flower called ironweed that was not yet blooming, though judging from the tiny purple buds becoming evident, they too would bloom any day.

Although the prairie was alive with color, we could anticipate a second round of splendor weeks later—one that would be nourished by late summer and fall rains. We saw the long serrated leaves of sawtooth sunflower, a tall yellow sunflower that blooms late in the fall, as well as several other species including aster and goldenrod that ride out the heat of summer, waiting for cooler weather to arrive before they flower. Some shine until the killing frosts of winter wilt their blooms and send them into the earth from which they came. And then the first spring beauties and crow poisons pop up in midwinter, bringing the prairie full circle.

As usual the child in me could not resist the urge to climb to the top of the mima mounds. Most were covered with an entanglement of vines with tiny thorns, spreading over, under, and around the prairie grasses. Often called blackberries, these bear the common name of dewberry, and people unfamiliar with them might mistake the red and purple berries for the fruits of different plants. However, a simple taste test would likely solve the misunderstanding. Bill and I dined on a couple of handfuls of ripe purple ones—a taste so instantly sweet that I felt a sudden burst of energy. It was a fitting way to end our day.

Our tour complete, we unloaded four small bales of prairie hay—bundles of Prairie Time bound tightly by wire—into my garden. I broke them open and spread them upon the ground. I wrapped the hay carefully around cultivated prairie plants to retain moisture in the soil and thus to nourish life even in death, as in the prairie. When the summer sun bakes the soil on hot days, the rich aroma of the prairie wafts upward into my nostrils, reminding me of a day of soul vacationing on a big prairie. Like the prairie's other ingredients of fire, water, and soil, the decaying grass gives life back to the earth, a natural part of the prairie's cycle of life.

SURVIVAL OF THE FITTEST

My ambition has been to succeed in redeeming Texas from
its wilderness state by means of the plough alone. . . . In
doing this I hoped to make the fortune of thousands and
my own amongst the rest.

Stephen F. Austin, 1829

It is plain, that our wide-spreading prairie pasture will soon
be gone; when we shall be forced to resort to the grass-
growing system, or our rich milk and butter and fat cattle
will be gone too. . . . Some of our more thoughtful farmers,
men whose minds and souls are not wholly engrossed
with the all-absorbing 'cotton, cotton first balle of
cotton," . . . are already beginning to speak of the waning
grass, before the prairies shall all be plowed up.

Gid (pseud.), *Texas Almanac*, 1861

"THE prairie *had* to be plowed, you know," I was once informed by a seasoned citizen from the Blackland, whose tone
suggested his knowledge of this fait accompli was the wisdom of
his years.

He felt I needed to be disabused of any romantic notions I might harbor about the prairie. The prairie had to be plowed because civilization demanded it. The wilderness had been eliminated so that everyone from yeoman farmers to captains of industry could partake of its riches. In this view, the rich prairie soil had been waiting for thousands of years, blooming profusely while it waited, ever so patiently, until the plows were at last thrust into it. Finally, freed of the need to be merely beautiful, the prairie could get on with what it was created to do in the first place — earn money for people. Nature's beauty had no intrinsic value unless it could be turned into commodities, the worth of which could be appraised. Buttressing the argument was the assertion that nature must be able to dish out the greatest good for the greatest number of people, or it was worthless.

This gentleman's view was like that of many other Blackland natives whose young lives were scarred by the Great Depression and then redeemed by the Second World War. The worst economic disaster in the history of the nation, the Great Depression was at its core a vortex sucking the American virtues of self-reliance and self-determination down the drain. With the economy free-falling after the stock market crash in 1929, many Americans were left feeling helpless and out of control. Even nature itself seemed to be conspiring against them as plowed up soil across much of the Great Plains began to blow away during the dust bowl.

Despite President Roosevelt's experimental intervention known as the New Deal, the age-old method of using plowshares to relieve suffering proved an ineffective means of conquering the wilderness of continuing hunger and joblessness. Historically, during hard times Americans had simply packed up and moved west in search of virgin lands to plow. Thus they escaped the economic woes that plagued the nation like clock-work—recurring on average every twenty years during the nineteenth century. During the Great Depression the urge to move west appeared once again, as John Steinbeck described in *The Grapes of Wrath*—but the virgin land was gone and so, too, was the hope of finding something better in the west.

Slowly the realization sank in that plows were no longer a cure-all. In fact, people began to realize that plows had probably helped create at least some of the suffering by putting more people on the land and creating an abundance of foodstuffs and other crops, leading to depressed prices for farmers. As this reality reached Washington, a novel twist using plows was devised. The New Deal included among its tentacles a program to dole out money to farmers to plow under their crops so that prices would rise. If too much food had been the problem, then perhaps destroying food would solve it, the New Dealers reasoned. Yet the economy still languished—in part because rampant unemployment had turned many middle-class wage earners into beggars unable to afford even basic necessities, such as buying food. In the late nineteenth century, these individual failures would have been passed off in Darwinian terms that glossed over any shortcomings in the economy and rationalized the problems as personal weaknesses. The strong survive, the argument went, and the weak are swept up from the floor and discarded like trash. They did not understand the sinister, and recently released, market forces that plagued those who were bent on getting rich quick from the land. But as long as there was more room out west, it really did not matter. As long as there was more land that could be taken, the problem would fix itself.

Cole Porter's portrayal of this impulse in the song *Don't Fence Me In,* performed in 1944 by Bing Crosby and the Andrew

Sisters, captures the very essence of this desire to move west. "I want to ride to the ridge where the west commences," Porter wrote. Another poignant line, considering how poverty-stricken America had been during the Depression, is even more to the point: "And I can't look at hovels and I can't stand fences." Although the frontier was gone, Americans were still celebrating it, as the refrain makes clear: "Oh, give me land, lots of land under starry skies above, don't fence me in."

But by the twentieth century, nature began fighting back against the onslaught of the plow, and Americans learned that it was time to pay the piper for plowing the land. Unlike for Dorothy in *The Wizard of Oz*, whose childlike dream to return home finally came true, there could be no going home. Across vast stretches of the Great Plains, severe drought led to enormous clouds of dust as plowed up dirt dried out and blew away. When rains did come, gully washers were the result: the rootless earth became liquid and simply vanished, leaving huge eroded scars that turned rolling hillsides into miniature canyons. The dust bowl was not as apparent on the Blackland Prairie as elsewhere, but eroded lands carved with washouts now punctuate once smoothly sloping hillsides and serve as earthen artifacts reminding us what happened to the prairie in the not so distant past.

Ironically, it was only during World War II—when Americans finally began to abandon their plowshare notions of economic prosperity and began beating plows into swords to defeat evil forces abroad—that those on the home front began to climb from the abyss of the Depression. When the soldiers returned home victorious, they never forget the simple lesson they learned during those years of depression and war: obstacles could be defeated through determination and force of will. Therefore, the way to defeat the cycle of poverty on the plains was to subdue nature once and for all. Doing so called for new strategies and new battle plans.

It was a far different world that emerged after the war. With no virginal western lands left to settle, people sought refuge in cities and towns, and universities, where they could expand the frontiers of business and industry. Never again would Americans celebrate the pastoral values of living *off* the land in agrarian utopias similar to those envisioned by Thomas Jefferson. According to Jefferson's view, an America peopled by independent small farmers would provide the best safeguards for liberty and democracy. Later generations, however, including my own, may now rhapsodize about living *on* the land, yet only a few hardy souls are willing to try living off the land in this age of instant gratification and consumerism.

Thus the twentieth century witnessed a different kind of movement, an exodus *from* the land, reversing an American journey that had begun almost three hundred years before. This time, the urges that drove people from the land were the same ones that almost a century earlier had led determined people— including young Stephen Austin—to search for riches by redeeming the wilderness. Although the journey from the land actually began after World War I, it culminated after World War II.

History seldom mentions the failed dreams that drove the pioneers back East, but the phenomenon was more common than textbooks would have us believe. What tornadoes and hailstorms failed to do, fires, insects, grasshoppers, drought, and loneliness would often accomplish. The Great Depression was one of a long train of events that drove people from the land. As always, those who remained and adapted to the changing world were praised because history celebrates winners, casting them as those whose survival was the result of their fitness. They are seen as the quintessential Americans—tough, hardy folk who survived by carving a home from the hostile wilderness. Such arguments have even been advanced concerning the plants and animals that once inhabited the prairies. They were doomed, according to this flawed reasoning, because they were unable to adapt to the decimation of the land they used for survival.

Like the pioneer accounts of the prairie's beauty and diversity that can be found buried in library archives, the reminders of these people who turned away from the land can still be found scattered all across the Blackland Prairie. Thousands of dying frame houses sag this way and that, slowly returning to the dirt. Open-air museum pieces tucked away on the edges of fields or crumbling next to dusty roads, they stand out amid the choking tall weeds and trees. Their steeply pitched roofs are usually open, allowing easy access to the Barn Owls and Black Vultures that seek shelter and seclusion in rooms where little children snuggled under blankets in unheated rooms on cold prairie nights. Yards where children may have played jacks or marbles are "growed up," hardy clumps of iris or antique roses still adorning transient ruins that for a few more years will bear witness to a time of hope on the prairie. Soon these rickety houses will be gone, like the prairie grasses that once ruled these gentle hills, and the wind will pass over a new landscape. People traveling by will little care or even remember those who changed the prairie landscape forever in a vain, brief attempt to find fortune there.

Yet, in abandoning the land and trying to remove themselves from the historic struggle that has always existed between people and their environment, they paved the way for even greater manipulation of nature. Although pretending to be removed from the wilderness altogether, they simply deferred the struggle onto others and forced those who remained in agriculture to pick up the slack. To compensate, farmers turned toward business and industry to survive—a move that required a heavier hand on the land through the use of chemical fertilizers and pesticides. Instead of flowers blooming, the spring smells that now permeate the nostrils are chemical in nature. Even when the windows are rolled up, the ubiquitous odors from the poisons seep inside our cars, while their deadly chemicals seep into our water, our soil, and the plants we consume. Sadly, there is no way to escape from this wilderness.

Although some of the people who grew up here and then moved on as young adults have retired closer to their roots, many have no desire to return—or to even contemplate an earlier reality here. This was a lesson I learned the hard way while speaking to a luncheon crowd at a small museum celebrating the cotton industry in Hunt County. To begin, I posed the question: "Who would like to be able to go back and see what this land looked like several hundred years ago?"

The response from one woman of that generation was so adamantly opposed to the idea that I felt assailed. She would certainly *not* like to go back, and the merest suggestion of the notion was almost unthinkable to her. It was a reaction I had not anticipated; I had failed to realize that my desire to use land and history to fuel imagination about the past were not shared by all. I was relieved to find that several people were after all interested and stayed late to ask questions and pass on tidbits of prairie lore. One, though, was the gentleman who felt compelled to remind me that the prairies had to be plowed.

But was the fellow right? Did the prairies have to be plowed? It is a question so fraught with emotion that answering it is akin to confessing that one's parents should not have had children. Asking if the prairies had to be plowed is rather like asking whether Lincoln had to be shot. The truth is that these things have happened, and we must now deal with the deck we have been dealt. I realized long ago that without the plows, without the hopeful pioneers, the sometimes desperate settlers, and the greedy masses aiming for easy money, I would not have been.

It is also important to recognize that to a very real extent, our standard of living today comes from the fact that we are freed from the toil of growing every morsel of our own food. The rich black soil that nourished the prairie and its early inhabitants still nourishes us today, though in return we destroyed the prairie, perhaps forever. But what we have done is make a trade. We traded a clean environment in which we had to labor ceaselessly for a poisoned one where the living was easy. But the new lifestyle came with a price as well—among its costs are higher rates of cancer and birth defects and other maladies. It is a process that will likely continue as genetically modified foods (including some that have in pesticides built into plant DNA) continue to replace those we have used for generations.

This will be our legacy to the land, unless we can find ways to reinvent the landscape on a grand scale somewhere, and replace the missing components, and clean up the land for those who come after us. We should not be allowed to fall back on the tired explanation that the disappearance of so many organisms was the result of their unfitness or their incompatibility with modern civilization. They are gone because someone willed it to be so.

STALKING THE WILD
PRAIRIE GRASS

The whole face of the country—bottom-lands, woodlands, and prairie uplands—is verdant with grass, which
suffers but little diminution in the winter.

David B. Edward, *The History of Texas*, 1836

Luckily in America, since fence we must, we discovered
cheap fencing while much of the country was still virgin,
and right-of-ways for rail and for automobile traffic were
securely fenced with the natural growths still intact. This
accident in our history has given us in effect a kind of wildlife preserve in elongated "relic areas," cutting across all
vegetational regions from every angle of approach, crisscrossing them so thoroughly that a listing would perhaps
include all or nearly all of the species present when the
white man first occupied the country.

Roy Bedicheck, *Adventures with a Texas Naturalist*, 1947

ON April 10, 1849, the sailing ship *Constitution* slipped out of
the busy port city of Liverpool, England, destined for New York.
On board were Edward Smith and John Barrow, two young
Englishmen with a scheme up their sleeve. Their final destination

was the vast remote prairies of northern Texas. It was here that they intended to stalk the wild prairie grasses in search of a large unclaimed tract that they hoped to acquire for a song. From the accounts they wrote, their journey has the feel of a safari, yet the men were not sightseers. Nor were they unwashed immigrants intent on leading a pastoral life in the virgin wilderness.

John was a civil engineer and Edward had plans to become a physician. Their objective, in purely capitalistic terms, was to make money—lots of money. What they wanted was forty leagues of undeveloped prairie—over 177,000 acres—which they hoped to finagle from the State of Texas for nothing. Like others with similar ideas, they planned to settle families, taking their payment in land for the improvements and assistance they would provide.

And so they headed to Texas, journals in hand, eager to take notes to "assist" potential colonists with the details they would need in order to relocate. Everything potential colonists should know would be included in their reports, which they published in London on their return. Especially important were information on the nature of soils and water and knowledge of native grasses and their uses.

The pair sailed into New York on the first of May, after a rough three-week journey across the Atlantic. Reaching Texas would be even more arduous, however, because there was no direct route. The trip would involve several routes and modes of transportation. The following day they departed for Albany via the Hudson River on the first leg of their journey. From Albany they headed west on the Albany and Buffalo Railroad before continuing by boat across Lake Eire to Michigan. Here they boarded another train—the Central Michigan Railroad—for Lake Michigan. After crossing the lake they journeyed along the Illinois Canal to the Illinois River. Once on the Mississippi River, they followed it south all the way to New Orleans—arriving in that bustling port city on the Gulf of Mexico on May 17.

In New Orleans Smith and Barrow had to board a steamboat for the four-day trip back up the Mississippi and into the Red River to reach Shreveport, Louisiana. After a short delay there to buy horses, they booked passage on a steamboat churning the dark waters up Big Cypress Bayou and winding through Caddo Lake's labyrinth of cypress trees draped with Spanish moss. Finally, on May 24, six weeks from home, the pair arrived in Jefferson, Texas.

In 1849 Jefferson was a booming river port and served as the gateway into northern Texas, both for people and for the supplies that made life easier for them. From there goods had to be hauled, laboriously and at great cost though, over undependable roads and in all sorts of weather. Next Smith and Barrow intended to visit the small hamlet known as Dallas on the banks of the Trinity River; but since there was no direct route, they were again forced to follow a circuitous one. The horseback ride from Jefferson to Dallas would take three weeks—as long as it had taken to cross the Atlantic Ocean.

Mounting their horses in Jefferson, the pair headed northwest along the main road to Daingerfield, a small town located in what was then the southeast corner of Titus County. The trails were dusty, and at times muddy, and the smells of earthy organic matter and the irrepressible odor of horse manure were their constant companions. They were exposed to the elements on all sides—a necessity that allowed them to experience the prairie and its people with great clarity.

Noting that the iron ore hillsides surrounding Daingerfield might someday prove valuable, Smith and Barrow continued northwest toward Mount Pleasant before turning east toward Hopkins County. They were most likely traveling along the old Caddo Indian trail that passed near the forgotten village of Daphne when they encountered their first glimpse of prairie— close to the Hicks family prairie that is still there.

Continuing east, they entered their first really large prairie— a massive opening in the forest known as White Oak Prairie, centered squarely on what is today the dairy country of Hopkins County—and were literally stopped in their tracks by the boundless beauty and the panoramic horizons. "Nature there," Smith wrote, "exists in a million forms to which we are strangers; and everywhere she clothes herself in beauty." He called this one of his favorite places in all of Northeast Texas, considering it one of four suitable locations for planting his mammoth colonization effort.

These were rich grasslands and would make a wonderful place to plant a settlement, Smith wrote. "The Wire-grass," he noted correctly, "almost exclusively, grows upon the prairies of Hopkins County. It is a narrow leaf growing three or four feet in height and the world cannot shew [sic] cattle in finer condition than those roaming uncared-for over these splendid prairies."

Smith provides a most telling revelation—breaking up the tough prairie sod would earn a laborer three dollars in cash per acre, or four dollars' worth of bartered goods. Today, the White Oak Prairie bears little resemblance to its former glory. All that is left of this sizable prairie near the headwaters of White Oak Creek are the tiny parcels sheltered by the Garrett family since the days of the Texas Republic. The mima mounds that once dotted the countryside like sesame seeds on a hamburger bun are mostly gone too—plowed under and buried beneath the soil, like the pioneers themselves.

A few miles later they approached Tarrant, the "county town" of Hopkins County, consisting "of twelve or fifteen houses congregated on a very large prairie, from which there is no line of separation." Nothing remains of Tarrant today, nearby Sulphur Springs having become the county seat.

From Tarrant they turned north toward Paris, crossing the forks of the Sulphur River and the grassy prairies that rose like mountain meadows above the wooded lowlands. The people who lived on these high prairies were healthier, Smith wrote, than those woodland dwellers subjected to the unhealthy vapors that rose from places where water stood about for months on end. They were fatter too, he insisted, than the scrawny lot whose misfortune it was to have chosen to live in the shade of the trees and not out on the abundance of the wide open prairie. Like a true promoter, Smith made it clear that the prairie offered the best choice for where to live.

Smith did caution prairie colonists not to place their homes in the middle of the prairie. Instead, a home site should be chosen next to a prairie in the shade of the woods. If either Smith or Barrow realized that such a location offered protection from the intense wildfires that raged across the prairie, neither of them dared mention a word about it.

In Paris they stopped to see the county clerk, who told them the county was filling up rapidly and the only "unlocated" prairie was a wire grass prairie west of town. I wonder how long this prairie remained before it vanished at the hands of someone who wanted to allocate it, someone who, like today's developers, saw undeveloped, unlocated land as wasteland and a chance to make some quick money. It is tempting to speculate that the relict wire grass prairie at the Gambill Goose Refuge may be part of the large tract the county clerk described to Smith.

While in Lamar County, the men noted the distinctive appearances of the two different prairie types that occur there. Smith commented that the wire grass prairies grew on sandy soil, but on the Blackland there was a grass called calamus. Calamus grass is almost certainly eastern gamagrass. In the mid-nineteenth century the word *calamus* was used to describe a reed, a stalk, or stubble—a description that closely matches the single erect stalk of this plant, especially in midsummer. Smith recorded that it remained green well into the winter, an accurate description as well.

From Paris the duo headed west toward Bonham and then Sherman, following the footsteps of Davy Crockett, who had taken the same trail a few years earlier. As they traveled west along the ridge where U.S. Highway 82 is located today, they may have passed right through the Smiley-Woodfin Meadow. They noted that its location would make an excellent location for the proposed Great Pacific Railroad because it would avoid many of the creeks and rivers and fewer bridges would have to be constructed.

A transcontinental railroad stitching the Atlantic and the Pacific and all the land between into a giant patchwork quilt had been the dream of railroad developers since the 1830s. Texans were intensely anxious to see such an undertaking succeed, provided of course that the railroad could be routed through Texas. Prior to the Civil War, however, talks on the matter stalled in Congress because a route could not be agreed upon. Northerners preferred a more northerly route while, predictably, southerners wished to see the line pass through their region.

A southerly route was preferable, Smith argued, as it would remain snow free during the winter. But what was more pressing for the development of Texas, he stressed, were local railroads that could be linked to the steamboat trade. "They have probably the finest agricultural and manufacturing country in the world," he wrote, "only requiring railroads to attract settlers with capital and enterprise, in order to develop it." Reflecting the view then in vogue concerning the role of railroads, Smith added that "should this Great Pacific Railroad not be secured to Texas, it is evident that one must be constructed to traverse the interior part of the northern prairies, and directly connect them with Lower Red River." A rail line from Shreveport to Bonham would do just that, he suggested, and would be the best way to develop the region.

The pair continued to Bonham and then Sherman before turning south toward and McKinney and finally Dallas. After a brief stay in Dallas, a crude frontier settlement in those days, they headed straight for Jefferson, where they boarded a vessel and returned to the Emerald Isle. Their dream colony would never materialize. Perhaps their funding fell through, or they became disenchanted with the notion of acquiring land and promoting it. As they pointed out, the lack of railroads in pre–Civil War Texas was certainly a limiting factor and may have played a role in their failure to follow through with their big ideas.

Following the Civil War, a new generation realized that it would take more than wild prairie grasses, or a knowledge of them, to make the country prosper. If the prairie were going to be redeemed from the wilderness, trade and transportation were as important as promoting the region to the world and devising schemes to attract people. This was still an isolated region, largely cut off from the rest of the world, and slowly civic boosters began to realize that it would take elbow grease and lots of money if large crowds were to be lured to the prairies. In short, it would take railroads. More than thirty years passed before the railroad Smith and Barrow suggested to link northeast Texas with the Red River would become a reality. Originally chartered in 1871, the East Line and Red River Railroad was planned to do just that—by connecting Jefferson directly with the proposed Katy Railroad when it reached Denison.

The proposed route of the railroad was unclear, but a direct route to Denison would have bypassed Greenville, the Hunt County seat of government. Greenville was a small collection of buildings isolated on a series of rolling prairie hillsides west of the narrow, shallow, and densely wooded river called the Sabine, just a few miles south of its headwaters. The town had grown only slightly since being organized and named the county seat in 1846. During rainy spells the Sabine would overflow its banks and flood the bottomlands, cutting off trade from the East. Residents hungered for a railroad, and in 1875, by offering inducements to the owners of the line, a group of townspeople successfully proposed that the East Line be diverted south to Greenville. I am sure they mentioned that by going west toward Greenville, the railroad could be built along the prairie ridge that separated the Sabine River watershed from that of the Sulphur River.

In 1876 workers began laying the narrow-gauge track northwest from Jefferson. Roughly following the well-worn trails taken by Smith and Barrow a quarter century earlier, the rail reached Daingerfield the following year and Sulphur Springs by 1879. From there it headed almost due west toward Greenville, tracking across the unplowed prairies and grazed pastures and through the small towns of Cumby and Campbell.

As the trains first arrived in Greenville in late 1880, I imagine few people noticed that the leaves on the prairie grasses along the route were beginning to curl and reveal their fall color. Taken for granted, too, were the purple fall asters and the decorative seed heads of rattlesnake master that waited for a passing animal to scatter them. In the excitement no one realized that in places the right-of-way would preserve a narrow slice of prairie—an unintended consequence of the railroad.

It is a transformation that I think of often, and now that we have moved to the land where I grew up, I again hear and feel the familiar deep rumbling of the train's diesel engines as they thunder past, shaking the ground like massive herds of buffalo. It is the land before the rails and the transformation they wrought, though, that I dream about when the shrill whistle wakes me up as it screams past in the middle of the night. As the trains rumble by carrying tractor-trailers preloaded with cargo coming to and from the Red River at Shreveport, I imagine the long-forgotten workers who put this railroad here. Between busily nailing the rails onto timbers dug into the earth, did they admire the tiny white prairie roses that emerge from the moist soil? Did they pause long enough to ponder the prairie hillsides that disappeared effortlessly toward the light blue horizon?

It is a view that I have tried to reconstruct in my mind many times as I have walked the ancient hills that slough off the ridge like carefully contoured modeling clay hardened and held in place by thick grass. The tip of one of these long linear hillsides lies within a century-old fence a quarter mile south of the tracks and delineates the northern boundary of our property. It is a grassy hillside, unplowed since the Great Depression but with the scars of disturbance still evident. Yet I love the land because a good number of prairie plants have returned, and it does not bear the botanical scars of recent plowing and is not choked by noxious pollen-producing weeds like western ragweed.

To most people these characteristics are invisible. Still, I like to think of this recovering hillside as a sign, a relic of past land usage, understood by those who speak the language of the grass. In places little bluestem has returned, but this alone does not make ours too different from thousands of other pastures that have been fallow for a few years. Several other tall grasses once again grace the slopes, and many bona fide prairie wildflowers have returned—including prairie clover and two different species of gayfeathers. One spring several years ago I even found a single bloom of purple coneflower, but though I have searched each year since then, I have not found it again. It was a thrill beyond measure one bright November day to happen upon a small colony of switchgrass clinging to life almost entirely under the shade of a tall cedar threatening to silence it.

What this hillside lacks is that carefully constructed order so apparent on a prairie. It is no longer an ancient community in which eastern gamagrass and switchgrass have learned to share the micro-depressions in the gilgai, where the moisture is greater, while Indiangrass and big bluestem thrive on the drier micro-ridges. What this land looked like eons ago—which plants arose from it and covered it like hair, which communities of grasses it hosted—are never-ending questions that I still ponder almost every day. The yearning to know was what drove me to become a stalker of wild prairie grasses in the first place.

I learned that the answers could not be found in books. So, armed with only a basic knowledge of a few wildflowers and even fewer grasses, I was determined to find out what a prairie looked like. My first experience came on Paul Mathews Prairie near Floyd one sultry June morning, and I was rudely awakened. Two species of purple coneflowers were dancing in the breezes, and the place seemed to be dominated by a grass I had never even seen and did not recognize. It was a lush experience, and it was clear that I had a lot to learn.

When I learned that this mystery grass was called eastern gamagrass, I began to wonder if it once grew on our land as well. The Houston Black soil on Paul Mathews Prairie is not as heavy, or as black, as the clay loam on our property, so it occurred to me that perhaps our land had hosted a slightly different grass community—one not so dominated by eastern gamagrass. This was my working hypothesis until I encountered the Garrett prairie near Miller Grove, whereupon I became even more confused.

The dominant there is Silveus's dropseed, another grass I could not identify, though I had seen it on other prairies. Because the soils there and on our property are similar, I reasoned that perhaps this was the grass that once flourished on our land. I tossed this theory around and around until I found the small prairie north of Commerce owned by Shelly Seymour's family. Eastern gama and wire grass were both growing there—the wire grass in neat little oval-shaped patches surrounded by eastern gamagrass. It was a remarkable learning experience. What I realized was that this piece of prairie history had preserved intact a small bit of evidence for how one prairie community collided into another. As the soil becomes sandier toward the bottom of the hill—and closer to Barnett Creek—wire grass becomes more common, leaving eastern gama to predominate on the thick black clay on the hillsides.

The following autumn I got an even better primer for how grass communities are related to soil. One clear blue October day Jerry Biggs, who starred in *Lonesome Dove*, invited me to visit a two-hundred-acre prairie owned by the family of a deceased friend. We also invited our mutual friend James Conrad, who is an archivist and historian at Texas A&M University–Commerce. A tall, scholarly individual, Jim understands the responsibility the prairies have in preserving our history and has become a crusader for protecting these valuable remnants. Besides writing a local newspaper column for years about the Blacklands, he has been preserving the scraps of paper on which early impressions of these prairies are recorded.

Located near Commerce, and just a little over a mile from Shelly's family's small prairie, this unplowed remnant is quite different. This prairie is on a soil called gray land by early pioneers (a name still in usage today), because it is a mix of black clay and sandy soil. It is often found on the eastern edge of the Blacklands—and as a community it has been overlooked by prairie ecologists. When we walked across the age-old landscape that October day, azure sage and big bluestem swayed in the breeze together, as they have done for thousands of years. What caught my attention was that eastern gama was completely absent, and although wire grass was common enough, it was not as abundant as it is on the Garrett family prairie. Stiff sunflower, one of the most common wildflowers nearby, was completely absent here.

Slowly, over many months and years, the answers are starting to come—and so are more questions. By examining the narrow corridors along nearby fences and along the railroad tracks, and looking at the soils, I am starting to understand what once grew here. But it is an imperfect knowledge—rather like selecting a few random pixels from the Mona Lisa and hoping to see the entire portrait. Poisonous herbicides have eliminated much of the diversity, and the problem is compounded by new landowners fond of bulldozing their fencerows. This insidious practice scrapes the earth bare, often removing as much as two feet or more of soil and completely eliminating the prairie grasses that cling to life there. These assaults on the last stands of prairie are repeated almost every time a "for sale" sign goes up or the land is chopped into smaller and smaller tracts.

Besides being a wholesale robbery of our natural heritage, this destruction makes it increasingly difficult to micromap the vegetation that once flourished in an area. Because plants may be tied to, or adapted to, specific soils, it is urgent that prairie enthusiasts and botanists take notes and collect seeds or even rescue the plants themselves if they are in danger of being destroyed.

Remarkably, after so many years, prairie treasures still await those eager enough to sleuth them out. Scattered here and there, they emerge each spring along county roads in out-of-the way places and even in the margins of highways. They can be located with a little bit of luck and a willingness to prepare for the encounter. Any old field full of tall grass, however, is not always going be a prairie. To recognize the real thing one needs to learn to read the signs—signs that are not obvious to most of us as we go about our business. It may be a stalk of gamagrass twisting in the wind that gives the game away, or a purple coneflower, or any of several other plants that are the telltale indicator species. If chance does indeed favor a prepared mind, then preparation and learning how to read the signs are imperative. Perhaps in so doing, we can help ensure that these forgotten, unmapped pieces of our botanical diversity will be discovered and loved back to life. It must be so if we are going to continue trying to understand the fragile world in which we live and the elusive past from which we come. But they must be found and they must be saved.

Today one of the "facts" most often repeated about the

Texas Blackland Prairie is that "fewer than five thousand acres remain." The estimate, however, was not based on the kinds of systematic surveys that geologists use to map oil reserves or that soil scientists and wildlife managers use to inventory resources under their care. The truth is that we have no idea how many acres of unplowed prairie grass remain in the Lone Star State. We have no idea because this kind of knowledge has never been profitable to business or useful to the academicians who provide the scientific background for such studies. Given our lack of knowledge, then, rigorous surveys should be conducted throughout each county known once to have supported these tall grasses. Besides all the high-tech tools, such as inspecting the terrain in satellite images, researchers seeking our prairie heritage should place a great deal of emphasis on landowners, county agents, and others who are, in the buzz-phrase of conservationists, "on the ground."

More than a few times when I have said the word *prairie* to someone, eyes have lit up and confessions have been elicited— "Oh yeah, Mr. So-and-So has a prairie," or "We had one, but we *had* to plow most of it." The frequency of these revelations is itself revealing, because it means that there are still prairies waiting to be shielded from an uncertain future. Each one should be preserved and urgently mapped with the same level of interest that is afforded a new tomb in Egypt's Valley of the Kings. Each one is too valuable to be passed off by conservationists as not big enough or too expensive. Yet, sadly, this is the fate destined for some of them.

Financing is a big concern. Without deep pockets, the grim reality is that the prairie remnants we find cannot all be protected through purchase. Yet, without education campaigns designed to arm landowners with a sense of stewardship for our prairie heritage, the matter of conserving additional prairie acreage may be a moot point. The people who own the prairie are those best placed to understand and safeguard its worth. Most others are probably like a student of mine, who confessed that she and her husband had followed the signs to Paul Mathews Prairie after hearing me talk about it. When they got there they found it disappointing, and they drove on by.

As she told her husband, "I don't see anything but grass . . ."

ISBN 1-58544-501-0